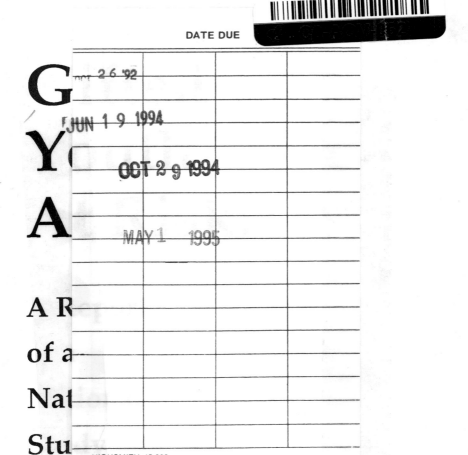

G

Y

A

A R

of a

Nat

Stu

Joyce VanTassel-Baska

James M. Patton

Douglas Prillaman

A Product of the ERIC Clearinghouse on Handicapped and Gifted Children

Published by The Council for Exceptional Children

LC
3993.9
.V36
1991

Library of Congress Cataloging-in-Publication Data

VanTassel-Baska, Joyce.
    Gifted youth at risk : a report of a national study / by Joyce
VanTassel-Baska, James M. Patton, Douglas Prillaman.
        p.   cm.
    Includes bibliographical references.
    ISBN 0-86586-206-0
    1. Gifted children--Education--United States--Evaluation.
2.   Gifted children--Education--United States--Statistics.
3.   Socially handicapped children--Education--United States-
-Evaluation.   4.   Children of minorities--Education--United States-
-Evaluation. I. Patton, James M.   II. Prillaman, Douglas.
III. Title.
LC3993.9.V36   1991
371.95--dc20   91-27494
                                                                   CIP

ISBN 0-86586-206-0

A product of the ERIC Clearinghouse on Handicapped and Gifted Children

Published in 1991 by The Council for Exceptional Children, 1920 Association
Drive, Reston, Virginia 22091-1589.
Stock No. P347

This publication was prepared with funding from the U.S. Department of
Education, Office of Educational Research and Improvement, contract no.
RI88062007. Contractors undertaking such projects under government
sponsorship are encouraged to express freely their judgment in professional and technical matters. Prior to publication the manuscript was
submitted for critical review and determination of professional compe-
tence. This publication has met such standards. Points of view, however,
do not necessarily represent the official view or opinions of either The
Council for Exceptional Children or the Department of Education.

Printed in the United States of America
10 9 8 7 6 5 4 3 2 1

Contents

1. **Who Are the At-Risk Gifted?**   3
   Two of the most neglected populations in gifted education are
   (1) economically disadvantaged, and/or (2) individuals whose
   talents may not be recognized or actualized because they are
   culturally diverse. These students are at risk: They are in danger of missing the benefits of educational services designed to
   nurture special abilities.

2. **Defining At-Risk**   5
   This study of state departments of education found great differences in philosophy and definitions of at-risk students.

3. **Identifying At-Risk Students**   11
   State directors perceived their states as embracing a broad conceptions of giftedness; however, the data reflected strong use
   of traditional approaches to identification.

4. **Differential Programming for At-Risk Students**   21
   Effective program interventions and current practices are reported.

5. **Creative Problem-Solving in Finding Funds**   37
   Categorical funding for at-risk students has not been
   considered a priority, but recently the Javits Gifted and
   Talented Education Act has provided an infusion of
   appropriated funds.

6. **Suggestions for a Working Agenda**   41
   The authors offer suggestions on identification, developing
   programs, and funding for at-risk gifted students

List of Tables and Figures

Acknowledgement

We would like to acknowledge the support of our colleagues, Virginia Laycock and Jack Nagle in the School of Education at the College of William and Mary, for their encouragement and help in this endeavor and its aftermath—Project Mandala. A special thank you to Cathy Prigge, Administrative Assistant for The Center for Gifted Education, for typing the manuscript and to Kris Bessemer, Elizabeth Boldrick, Megan Fettig, Ann Weaver, and Barbara Zaremba for their assistance in preparing tables and locating references.

Preface

Issues concerning underrepresented populations of gifted students have long been a concern of The Council for Exceptional Children. Philosophical and pragmatic dilemmas such as identification and programming for highly able youth who might not have an opportunity to develop their potential are particularly troublesome. Some of the factors that enter into identification—cultural diversity, low SES, geographic isolation—are currently being addressed by the field of gifted education. Impetus has been provided not only by general concern, but also by the Javits Education Act of 1988 (P.L. 100-297). The Javits Act provided limited funding for a National Research Center and projects designed to "plan, conduct, and improve programs for the identification and education" of these students.

CEC/ERIC is particularly pleased to present this volume as a contribution to the literature on identification practices and programs for students who tend to be underrepresented in gifted programs. The authors have provided readers with information on effective program interventions and practices. They offer a variety of suggestions on identification, developing programs, and funding.

Sandra L. Berger
Staff Editor

Introduction and Purpose of the Study

Concern for some culturally diverse and economically disadvantaged gifted learners prompted the authors to explore the nature and extent of programs and services available for these populations. The study was organized around the following areas of inquiry:

1. Determining the philosophical and definitional considerations used to address these special populations of gifted learners;

2. Determining the major approaches used by the states to identify and provide programs for these students;

3. Determining the level and extent of state funding patterns, policies, procedures, and program standards; and

4. Comparing results with national data based on poverty levels, student race and ethnicity, geographical location, and size of population.

The study, conducted during the mid-1980s, was organized in three phases.

1. A questionnaire was sent to all 50 states and U. S. territories seeking answers to the above areas of inquiry.

2. A questionnaire was sent to a selected group of local districts that have active programs for at-risk gifted learners.

3. A series of 12 case studies probed the nature of exemplary programs for these learners across the United States.

This monograph reports the results gleaned from Phases one and two of the study and offers a comprehensive review of the current knowledge about programs and services for some gifted students who are culturally diverse or economically disadvantaged.

1. Who Are the At-Risk Gifted?

Two of the most neglected populations in gifted education are individuals whose talents may not be recognized or actualized because they are (1) culturally different from the mainstream culture, and/or (2) economically disadvantaged. School districts that use achievement scores to identify gifted youth for special programs frequently overlook these youngsters. Standards for program entry are often above the students' tested achievement levels. Even when such students are found and placed in programs, little attention is given to socioeconomic or cultural factors that may negatively affect their performance in special programs and their future achievements beyond such programs. These students are at risk: They are in danger of missing the benefits of educational services designed to nurture special abilities. Consequently, the following questions merit attention:

1. Why are these students at risk of failing to be identified as gifted?

2. Why are these students at risk of not benefitting from traditional special programs?

3. What provisions can be made to minimize the risk of inappropriate identification practices and ineffective programming?

FAILURE TO BE IDENTIFIED AS GIFTED

Studies have shown that most students identified as gifted come from above average socioeconomic backgrounds (Sears & Sears, 1980; VanTassel-Baska & Willis, 1987). There is a clear underrepresentation of minority students, particularly Hispanic-American and African-Americans, in gifted programs at the K-12 level of schooling (Baldwin, 1985).

A 1988 study commissioned by the United States Department of Education cited the following statistics about conditions in our schools, confirming the need to address this special group of gifted learners:

- Minority students are underrepresented in programs designed to serve gifted and talented students. Although minorities comprise 30 percent of public school enrollment, they represent less than 20 percent of the students selected for gifted and talented programs;

- Whereas students from low-income backgrounds comprise 20 percent of the student population, they make up only four percent of students who perform at the highest levels on standardized tests (those who score at the 95th percentile or above);

- High school seniors from disadvantaged families (in which the mother did not complete high school) are less than half as likely to have participated in gifted and talented programs as more advantaged seniors; and

- Disadvantaged students are far less likely to be enrolled in academic programs that can prepare them for college and are about half as likely to take coursework in advanced math and science than more advantaged students. Only two percent of high school seniors from poor families take calculus, whereas approximately seven percent of those from more advantaged backgrounds do (Alamprese, Erlanger, & Brigham, 1988).

In 1985, culturally diverse students represented nearly 20% of the public school population. In the same year, approximately 31% of African-Americans and 29% of the Hispanic-American population were below poverty level (United States Bureau of the Census, Statistical Abstract of the United States, 1987). While highly visible in drop-out, teen pregnancy, and special education demographics, these students continue to be underrepresented in programs for the gifted and college bound.

2. Defining At-Risk

Gifted students from culturally diverse backgrounds and low socioeconomic environments may represent untapped potential. State departments of education and local school systems are challenged to identify and provide qualitatively different programs for the general gifted learner population. But defining, identifying, and developing program interventions for gifted minority, low socioeconomic, and those with disabilities pose even greater challenges. This national study of state departments of education found great differences and contradictions in philosophy and definition.

A questionnaire asked state directors of gifted programs to indicate the extent to which their gifted programs reflected principles of equality and pluralism. Forty-five percent (21) of those responding indicated that their state programs reflected principles of equality and pluralism at a moderate level; 23.1% (12) reported concerns for pluralism and equality to a "great extent"; 17.3% (9) reported "a lot"; and 9.6% (5) reported "little or no concern" for these factors.

Table 1 depicts the use of factors of "disadvantagement" in state definitions for gifted students. The largest percentage of the responding states (43%) lacked provision for considering disadvantagement in the state definitions. Of those who defined disadvantagement, 32.7% (17) used cultural difference as the determinant. Although states reported ethnicity as the most frequently used factor while identifying students for gifted programs, only nine included this factor. Fourteen states included socioeconomic factors in their definitions, 13 used linguistic factors, and 12 considered environmental factors.

Although states have been consistent in their philosophical support of economic, social, cultural, and racial diversity, they have moved slowly to incorporate these concerns into the definitional structures of their gifted programs. Given the present and projected increase of culturally and racially diverse student populations and students from low socioeconomic backgrounds in public schools, the lack of confluence between philosophy and use requires attention. State Departments of Education must create definitions and programs that are consistent with their philosophies.

STATE PROGRAM STANDARDS

The state study identified some important trends and issues regarding services provided for at-risk gifted learners. The data suggest that states have remained somewhat conservative about operationalizing a new concept of giftedness (beyond general intellectual ability as discerned through IQ and achievement testing). More than 16 years ago (Marland, 1972), the field of gifted education officially embraced an expanded view of categorical identification. The limited movement by the states in that direction is surprising. New theoretical models and research published in the early 1980s lent additional credibility to an expanded vision of giftedness

TABLE 1
Factors of "Disadvantagement" Used in State Definitions

	1	2	3	4	5	6	7
AL							
AK							x
AZ				x	x		
AR							x
CA		x	x	x	x	x	
CO				x	x		
CT							
DE		x		x	x		
DC							
FL		x	x	x	x	x	
GA							x
HI							x
ID	x						
IL							x
IN					x		
IA							x
KS		x	x	x	x	x	
KY			x		x	x	
LA							
ME							x
MD	x						
MA			x	x	x	x	
MI					x	x	
MN							x
MS		x	x	x			
MO							x
MT							x
NE					x		
NV		x	x	x	x	x	
NH							x
NJ							
NM							x
NY							x
NC		x	x		x		
ND							x
OH							x
OK							x
OR			x	x	x	x	
PA							
RI							x
SC							x
SD			x				
TN							
TX	x						

TABLE 1 *(continued)*
Factors of "Disadvantagement" Used in State Definitions

	1	2	3	4	5	6	7
UT	x						
VT							x
VA		x	x	x	x	x	
WA		x	x		x		
WV			x	x			
WI							x
WY			x		x		
GU							x
PR							

1 = No response
2 = Environmental factors
3 = Socioeconomic factors
4 = Linguistic factors
5 = Cultural factors
6 = Ethnicity
7 = No inclusion

(Feldman, 1983; Gardner, 1983; Renzulli, 1978; Sternberg, 1985). State standards for administering programs and services have not kept pace with this work.

Three questions elicited information on statewide program standards. Respondents were asked (1) if state-developed program standards existed, and the degree to which the standards were the same for all gifted students; (2) if any initiatives were in place to monitor local education agency programs; (3) if they had developed special materials, handbooks, or guidelines.

Program standards for the at-risk gifted population are limited; generic standards for gifted programs have, in some states, been in place for less than seven years. Only one state has developed specific standards regarding services to this population. No states indicated that they have developed separate program standards for at-risk gifted students; 53.1% (26) responded "no" when asked this question. The largest percentage of respondents, 44.9% (22) indicated that their program standards were the same for at-risk and advantaged gifted students.

The data indicated that 82.7% of the states (43) employ no initiatives to monitor LEA implementation of programs for at-risk gifted students. However, 17.3% (9) indicated that initiatives existed to monitor local programs for the inclusion of at-risk gifted students in the gifted program.

Several states refer to the at-risk gifted in their state plans. Mississippi does not mandate programs, but local education agencies may design programs for four distinct populations—intellectually gifted, talented, gifted handicapped, and "disadvantaged" gifted. The State Department of

Education (SDE) provides a specific definition of the gifted at-risk population. The regulations for approved programs and criteria for the classification of gifted and talented students and "culturally and educationally deprived" students in Nebraska, cite program criteria and selection procedures as two areas where specific guidelines are to be followed. Within the program criteria, LEAs must provide evidence of planning to "assure access to programs by members of minority or educationally disadvantaged groups" (p. 4). The selection procedures section of Nebraska's regulations specify that "instruments and criteria shall be chosen to reflect the emphasis of the differentiated curriculum to be provided and to protect members of minority or educationally disadvantaged groups from test bias discrimination" (p. 6). Minnesota standards require that all instruments and procedures must be examined for cultural bias and "efforts must be employed to ensure the representation and participation of all student populations in gifted and talented educational programs to include individuals of all races, creeds, national origins, gender, physical handicaps, or economic status" (p. 6).

LOCAL SCHOOL DISTRICT PROGRAMS

Phase one of this study provided a general picture of services to at-risk gifted learners across the country. Phase two, a survey of local school districts, provided additional information. Fifty-one local districts responded to a survey developed by the authors. These districts were nominated by their state directors of gifted programs based on their program activity for at-risk gifted learners. Thus, the results are important for understanding the nature and quality of services currently in place.

Seventy percent (39) of the local districts responding indicated that they used a working definition of at-risk gifted learners. Definitions ranged from broadly-defined individual needs, to focus on a particular minority group prevalent in the school district, to multifaceted definitional structures that considered socioeconomic status (SES), cultural diversity, and linguistic factors.

A subsequent question on "factors involved in disadvantagement" showed that a majority (60%) used environment, SES, linguistic/cultural differences, and ethnicity. Of those responding, 43.8% used eligibility for free or reduced lunch as the SES determinant. Table 2 shows the districts, by number and percent, that used differential factors to determine the students who received services under the label "disadvantaged" gifted.

Only 12 districts indicated they had a definition of at-risk gifted learners; of those, nine reported a definitional construct. Four included culturally diverse, minority, and the poor in their definitions. Two sample definitions are:

1. Those children regardless of race or ethnic group who may have language patterns and experiences, cultural backgrounds, economic disadvantages, and/or educational disadvantages or differences which make it difficult for them to demonstrate their potential using traditional identification procedures (Prince George's County, MD).

TABLE 2
Number and Percentage of Factors Used in
Defining "Disadvantaged" Gifted Students
in Identified Local School Districts

Factor	Number	Percentage
Socioeconomic	35	68
Cultural	31	60
Ethnicity	31	60
Environmental	28	54
Linguistic	28	54
Other	6	12

Note: N = 51

2. Intellectually gifted children and youth are those who have potential for outstanding performance by virtue of superior intellectual abilities. Intellectually gifted means outstanding performance or potential for outstanding performance by virtue of superior intellectual abilities (K.A.R. 91-12-22 [q]). Both those with demonstrated achievement and those with minimal or low performance who give evidence of high potential in general intellectual ability, specific academic aptitudes, and/or creative thinking abilities are included in this definition (Garden City USD #457, KS).

A recent three-year study of key demographic features of at-risk gifted learners in the Midwest defined disadvantagement in purely economic terms (VanTassel-Baska & Willis, 1987). Large-scale sociological studies have focused on consideration of a father's education and occupational status as the key variables (Jencks, 1972). Other recent efforts in the field of gifted education focused on minority status and cultural difference as important variables in defining the term (Baldwin, 1985; Frasier, 1989). Since these variables can occur singly or in combination, no one definition appears to be clearly accepted by the field (Baldwin, 1985). The result of variance can be seen in the State of California omnibus definition of at-risk gifted (California Administrative Code 5-A, Sec. 3823D), which includes environmental, economic, cultural, language, and social factors.

Studies of at-risk gifted populations based on the omnibus definition have focused on the need to:

1. Use nontraditional measures to identify at-risk students (Bernal & Reyna, 1974; Bruch, 1978; Frasier, 1979; Torrance, 1971).

2. Recognize cultural attributes and factors in deciding identification procedures (Baldwin, 1985; Gay, 1978; Hilliard, 1976; Miller, 1974; Samuda, 1975; Witty, 1978).

3. Focus on strengths in nonacademic areas, particularly in creativity and psychomotor domains (Bruch, 1975; Hilliard, 1976; Torrance, 1977).

4. Create programs that address noncognitive skills, and programs that enhance motivation (McClelland, 1978; Moore, 1978).

The findings from this study support the following recommendations.

• States should adopt an omnibus definition of at-risk gifted that gives equal and separate consideration to low socioeconomic status and race/ethnic background.

• Local districts should systematically screen all students entering kindergarten who (a) are eligible for free or reduced lunch, or (b) come from minority backgrounds, for signs of academic promise. A pool of these students should be created for establishing early intervention programs and services leading to inclusion in gifted programs.

• Program standards should be developed that consider differential provisions for at-risk gifted learners. These standards need to become part of state regulations for gifted programs.

3. Identifying At-Risk Students

PHILOSOPHICAL ISSUES

Several philosophical approaches are associated with identification and intervention of at-risk gifted learners. The first approach is *equality of treatment.* Many states reported no difference in either identification or intervention for the at-risk gifted when compared to other gifted learners. Their procedures often reflect the notion that equal treatment is legally and politically the most appropriate strategy. This mode of thinking may have several strands. The first strand argues that the goal of a gifted program is to educate leaders for American society; thus, mainstream culture and values must be assimilated to participate in realizing that goal. A second strand argues that gifted programs should educate for "giftedness" regardless of other factors; thus, other kinds of differences should be minimized in favor of best practices for a population of learners based on their discernible advanced development. A third strand holds that differentiating identification or program standards based on low SES or race is an insult to the youngsters and ultimately serves them poorly in an educational sense.

A second approach, *equity through affirmative action,* contends that minority students should be included in gifted programs at a level commensurate with their representation in the general population. Some states and local school districts agree with this idea in principle and may even meet established quotas; yet they may not provide students with support mechanisms for retention and success in gifted programs. Systematic study to provide hard data on this issue is needed. Because traditional measures have not identified these students in appropriate numbers, both traditional and nontraditional instruments and selection processes should be used to meet equity goals.

A third approach, the principle of *individualization,* is deeply ingrained in the philosophy of gifted education. In this context, differentiation in identification and intervention would occur most naturally at the level of an individual child, not at the level of an ethnic group or SES category. The purpose of individualization is development of the child based on his present behaviors, predilections, and needs—not those of a sociopolitical context. The child's personal needs, rather than group membership, determine educational services.

Most state directors of gifted programs hold to the first and third perspectives as the principal means for interpreting provisions for at-risk gifted learners. These perspectives also affected the interpretation of the study.

State directors perceived their states as adopting a "moderate" position toward a broadened concept of giftedness regarding identification issues (mean = 3.3 on a scale of 5). However, the full range of responses to this item reflected much state-to-state variation. Only 22 states reported an extensive use of a broadened definition.

IDENTIFICATION PRACTICES

Table 3 shows that slightly more than 30% (16) of the responding states used low socioeconomic status (SES) "a lot" or "to a great extent" in identifying students for gifted programs; 34.6% (18) used this variable "a little" or "not at all." Moderate use of low SES was reported by 25% (13) of the states responding to the survey.

The table also shows the extent to which states included the variable of race or ethnicity to identify students for gifted programs: 28.9% (15) used this factor "to a great extent" or "a lot," 34.7% (18) responded "not at all" or "a little," and 26.9% (14) indicated moderate use. It is interesting that 11 states indicated they did not include race. This is significant because race is historically recognized as a significant factor in developing assessment techniques that uncover hidden talents among at-risk learners (Baldwin, 1987; Baska, 1989).

Some combination of race and low SES was used "a little" by 15 states (28.8%); ten states (19.2%) reported moderate use; and four states (7.7%) indicated the use of this amalgam "a lot" or "to a great extent." Twelve states (23.1%) did not use the combined factors at all.

TABLE 3
State Responses to Variables Used to
Identify Students for Gifted Programs

Extent of Variable Used	Low SES Frequency	%	Race Frequency	%	Race & Low SES Frequency	%
Not at All	10	19.2	11	21.2	12	23.1
A Little	8	15.4	7	13.5	15	28.8
Moderately	13	25.0	14	26.9	10	19.2
A Lot	12	23.1	11	21.2	4	7.7
To a Great Extent	4	7.7	4	7.7	4	7.4

Note: Percentages do not add to 100% because of no response from five states or territories. N = 47

States using low SES in their identification process were asked the basis upon which they defined low socioeconomic status. Of the 19 states responding, 42.1% (8) stated that student qualification for free or reduced lunch was the basis for determining low SES. An equal number responded that "other factors" were used in their definition. Three of the eight states who identified "other factors" in their definition allowed local school systems to make this determination; two states used state public assistance regulations and guidelines. The remaining three states who responded "other factors" indicated they lacked specific criteria. One state used the Bureau of Labor Statistics *Qualification for Aid to Families with Dependent Children* (U. S. Department of Labor, 1984) as the basis for defining low SES; two states used the Bureau's *Table of Income Based on Household Size* (United States Department of Commerce, 1980).

Although most states do not have data on the number of at-risk gifted students served, several states report some estimates by racial or ethnic categories. In Florida, 5,202 culturally diverse students (Black non-Hispanic, Asian, and American-Indian) are receiving services in programs for the gifted and talented. Approximately 35% of the gifted students in California are members of minority groups; however, the number of low-income at-risk students is unknown.

Table 4 reflects the extent to which states used indices that purport to identify constructs or types of ability, other than academic, in their identification of at-risk students. Creativity indices and use of products were most frequently employed (used by 39 and 37 states respectively). Outside experts were employed slightly less extensively. More than 90% of the states use norm-referenced tests to some extent to identify the at-risk gifted population.

TABLE 4
Nontraditional Indices of Ability
Used by States in Descending Order

Indices	# of States Using	# of States Not Using	No Response
Creativity Measures	39	3	5
Student Products	37	6	4
Expert Evaluation	35	6	6
Leadership	33	9	5
Adaptive Behavior	30	10	7
Case Study	29	11	7
Learning Style Inventories	29	12	6
Psychometric Inventories	16	25	6

Note: N = 47

All states indicated some use of nonbiased assessment techniques. Yet when queried further regarding specific aspects of nonbiased assessment protocols that might be employed, extent of use dropped dramatically. Nonbiased assessment protocols employ nontraditional tests, or use different norming standards for an existing test. However, 48.1% of the states indicated "little or no use" of such techniques; and only 19.2% indicated "a little use" of nonbiased assessment techniques.

These responses may be interpreted in several ways:

1. Respondents may not be familiar with the specific components of a nonbiased assessment protocol (even though they reacted affirmatively to the terminology);

2. Respondents viewed techniques such as observation by teachers and parents as more descriptive of "nonbiased assessment," or

3. The data on overall use of nonbiased assessment techniques was greater than actual use data collected from examination of individual components of an identification system.

The data reflected strong use of traditional approaches to identifying at-risk gifted students (88.5% of respondents indicated use of norm-referenced tests; 90.4% used teacher nominations). No other techniques were used so extensively. The limited numbers of at-risk students in gifted programs suggest that greater use of nontraditional measures is needed to identify this population. All states who responded to the item reported some use. Twelve states reported use of some additional procedures, varying considerably from state-to-state. No pattern of use emerged.

There was considerable variance among states regarding the role of individuals in identifying the at-risk gifted learner. As noted in Table 5, the most frequently used form of individual identification was teacher nomination, followed in descending order by parent, self, community, and peers.

TABLE 5
Role of Individuals in the Identification Schema for
At-Risk Gifted Students, by Degree

	A Lot To a Great Extent	Moderately	A Little To Not at All	No Response	Total
Teacher	34	6	3	4	47
Parent	21	13	9	4	47
Community	13	9	20	5	47
Self	7	21	15	4	47
Peer	7	18	18	4	47

Note: N = 47

LOCAL SCHOOL DISTRICT PROGRAMS

Just over 27% of the respondents reported that more than 20% of their participating gifted students were identified as at-risk. This data is somewhat misleading, since twenty-four districts (48%) did not respond to this question. Table 6 shows the number and percentage of students served in these local programs.

TABLE 6
Number and Percentage of At-Risk Gifted
Students Served in Local Districts

Percentage of At-Risk Served	Number of Districts	Percentage of Districts
0 - 5%	6	12
6 - 10%	2	4
11 - 15%	2	4
16 - 20%	3	6
Over 20%	13	26
No data reported	24	48

Note: N = 42

The study examined the use of identification measures other than IQ and achievement test results (Table 7). Ninety percent of the respondents indicated that nontraditional assessment was used to some extent. Those most frequently used were: nominations by teachers (87.5%), parents (68.8%), nontraditional test measures (52.1%), and student products (54.2%). Most frequently cited nontraditional identification measures were the Ravens Progressive Matrices (5) and the Kaufman-ABC (3). Locally developed scales were most frequently used (9) in the area of observation of children by adults. Some districts (3) used all or portions of the Renzulli Scales (Renzulli, Smith, White, Callahan, & Hartman, 1976). Most districts (7) reported use of the Torrance Test of Creative Thinking in some manner for creativity indices. The most frequently used (10) norm-referenced tests were traditional in-grade standardized achievement tests. A few districts (3) used the Cognitive Abilities Test.

Table 7 shows the number and percent of districts using these techniques to identify at-risk gifted students. Other measures (not shown in Table 7) were reported by fewer than 15% of the respondents.

TABLE 7
Techniques for Identifying Students At Risk By
Number and Percentage in Descending Order of Frequency

Instrument	Number	Percentage
Teacher Nomination	45	87.5
Parent Nomination	35	68.8
Nontraditional Testing	28	54.2
Student Products	27	52.1
Creativity Indexes	24	47.9
Observation	23	45.8
Self-Nominations	20	39.6
Norm-Referenced Tests	20	39.6
Peer Nomination	16	31.3
Community Nomination	9	18.8
Leadership Skills Inventory	9	18.8
Case Studies	6	12.5
Behavioral (Adaptive) Identification	4	8.3
Psychomotor Skill Inventory	3	6.3

Note: N = 51

NONTRADITIONAL APPROACHES TO IDENTIFICATION

One nontraditional approach to identification is to augment procedures with parent, teacher, or community checklists that include special characteristics of culturally diverse students who have been identified as gifted. Torrance (1969), for example, lists 18 "creative positives" to look for among African-American learners:

1. Ability to express feelings and emotions.

2. Ability to improvise with commonplace materials and objects.

3. Articulateness in role playing, sociodrama, and storytelling.

4. Enjoyment of and ability in visual arts, such as drawing, painting, and sculpture.

5. Enjoyment of and ability in creative movement, dance, dramatics, and so forth.

6. Enjoyment of and ability in music, rhythm, etc.

7. Use of expressive speech.

8. Fluency and flexibility in figural media.

9. Enjoyment of and skills in group activities, problem solving, and so forth.

10. Responsiveness to the concrete.

11. Responsiveness to the kinesthetic.

12. Expressiveness of gestures, body language, and so forth, and ability to interpret body language.

13. Humor.

14. Richness of imagery in informal language.

15. Originality of ideas in problem solving.

16. Problem centeredness or persistence in problem solving.

17. Emotional responsiveness.

18. Quickness of warm-up.

In related efforts, Hilliard (1976) and Anderson (1988) argue convincingly for the recognition of the powerful influence of culture and cultural systems on cognitive style and behavior. They identify characteristics of African-American learners that must be addressed, not merely in the identification process, but also in the development of curricula and the total instructional process. Some of the learning preferences they find characteristic of African-American learners are:

1. Emphasize group cooperation.

2. Value harmony with nature.

3. Accept affective expression.

4. Holistic or gestalt thinkers.

5. The field is perceived as responding to the person and may have a life of its own.

6. Use of strong, colorful expressions.

7. Relevant concepts must have special or personal relevance to the observer.

8. Language dependent upon unique context and upon many interactional characteristics of the communicants on time and place, on inflection, muscular movements, and other nonverbal cues.

9. Learning of material that has a human social content and is characterized by fantasy and humor (Anderson, 1989)

10. Perceived conceptual distance between the observer and observed.

Bernal & Reyna (1974) identified the following as typical of gifted Hispanic-American children:

1. Rapidly acquires English language skills once exposed to the language and given an opportunity to use it expressively.

2. Exhibits leadership ability, be it open or unobtrusive, with heavy emphasis on interpersonal skills.

3. Has older playmates and easily engages adults in lively conversation.

4. Enjoys intelligent (or effective) risk taking behavior, often accompanied by a sense of drama.

5. Is able to keep busy and entertained, especially by imaginative games and ingenious applications, such as getting the most out of a few simple toys and objects.

6. Accepts responsibilities at home normally reserved for older children, such as the supervision of younger siblings or helping others do their homework.

7. Is "street wise" and is recognized by others as a youngster who has the ability to "make it" in the Anglo-dominated society.

To identify minority students for gifted programs, Frasier (1989) calls for the following:

1. Use multiple criteria that include inventories and checklists that correspond to traits found in gifted minority populations.

2. Use the diagnostic-prescriptive teaching approach to improve test performance, popularized by Feuerstein's (1979) notion of test-teach-test.

3. Broaden the data-finding procedures for students, including approaches such as peer nomination, self-nomination, and assessments of other personnel in addition to teachers.

4. Consider broader ranges of scores for entrance into programs.

5. Use standardized tests that have a history of effectiveness in identifying at-risk students.

RECOMMENDATIONS

- It is imperative that state and local educational agencies adopt justifiable approaches to identifying at-risk gifted learners. Students in low income and minority groups who show promise on standardized measures should be considered for special programming.

- States should recommend a variety of identification measures that consider at-risk gifted learner profiles: (1) test scores on traditional and nontraditional measures, (2) actual performance in gifted-level classroom activities, and (3) recommendations from key personnel. Individual programming decisions need to be made through a team approach that considers all available options.

- We should consider carefully the match between selection criteria and programming. We should not exclude students who could succeed in a program by arbitrarily establishing cut-off scores that are unreasonably high. Evidence suggests that lowering entrance scores in a rigorous program with well-defined expectations neither affects the student success rate appreciably nor affects the overall standards of the class (Olszewski, Kulieke, Willis, & Krasney, 1987).

4. Differential Programming for At-Risk Students

Too many culturally diverse and low SES students reside outside the mainstream networks that provide knowledge about how to take advantage of educational opportunities. This knowledge is crucial to converting high aspirations into creative productive achievement. But it is not enough to provide students with such knowledge; empowering families with information and skills that link their children to available resources is crucial. Schools are responsible for providing direct service programs for at-risk gifted learners. Many lack information about the process of talent development and therefore cannot disseminate knowledge or provide resources. Thus, talented at-risk gifted children may not receive the benefits of special programs designed for gifted youth.

The section on intervention in the state questionnaire examined ways in which programs served at-risk gifted students. Most states (40) did not differentiate programs or services at all, or only "a little." Ten states provided no data on program intervention approaches.

Table 8 includes a "0" code above those program approaches found in the literature to be most effective with at-risk populations. This code distinguishes them from interventions frequently used with gifted populations, but not typically viewed as special intervention programs for some culturally diverse and economically disadvantaged students. The study revealed greater use of traditional program delivery models and less use of program approaches purported to be successful with at-risk gifted students. Only mentorships and creative programs are used by more than half the states. The results in Table 8 must be interpreted as overlaying general program approaches for serving all types of gifted students.

LOCAL SCHOOL DISTRICTS

The school district study identified approaches to programming with at-risk learners. Table 9 summarizes these approaches. More than half the respondents use at least one of the following program approaches: core academic programs in selected content areas, acceleration, process skill development, and creative programs. However, fewer than half use early intervention, counseling, individual tutorials, mentorships, internships, arts programs, academic skill development, test-taking skills, nontraditional placements, or independent study—even though many of these interventions are cited in the review of the literature (see pp. 29-36) as effective program interventions with at-risk students.

When asked to identify the grade levels served, 60.4% of those responding reported programs for at-risk gifted learners at the K-1 level. The percentage increased to 79.2% at grades 2-3, and leveled off at 64.6% in grades 11-12. Districts were also asked about differences in programs and services. Only five programs (10.5%) reported that "different services"

TABLE 8
An Overview of Intervention Programs for
At-Risk Gifted Learners by State

	01	02	03	04	05	06	07	08	09	10	11	12	13	14	15	16	17
AK	x	x	x	x	x		x	x	x					x	x		
AZ	x																
AR	x	x	x	x	x	x		x	x	x	x	x	x	x	x		
CA	x	x	x	x	x	x	x	x	x	x	x	x	x	x	x	x	
CO	x	x	x		x		x		x		x	x	x	x			
CT					x		x	x	x	x				x	x		
DE							x	x									
FL	x	x	x		x	x	x	x	x	x	x	x	x	x	x	x	
GA																x	
GU	x	x					x	x		x							
HI	x	x		x			x	x		x	x	x	x	x	x		
ID																x	
IL		x	x									x	x				
IN	x	x		x	x		x	x		x		x	x	x	x		
IA																	x
KS		x	x		x		x	x	x	x	x	x	x	x	x		
KY	x	x	x	x	x	x	x	x	x	x	x	x	x	x	x		
LA	x	x	x	x	x		x	x	x	x	x	x	x	x	x		
ME																x	
MD	x	x	x	x	x	x	x	x	x	x	x	x	x	x			
MA		x	x	x	x	x	x	x	x					x	x		
MI	x	x	x	x	x		x		x		x			x			
MN		x	x	x	x	x	x	x		x	x	x	x	x	x	x	
MS		x					x	x	x	x				x	x		
MO		x	x	x	x	x	x	x	x				x	x	x		
MT		x		x	x		x	x	x	x							
NE	x	x	x	x	x				x	x	x				x		
NV		x			x	x				x				x			
NH																x	
NM																	
NY		x		x	x	x	x	x		x		x	x	x	x		
NC		x		x	x	x	x	x	x	x	x	x	x	x	x		
ND																x	
OH		x	x		x			x	x		x			x	x	x	
OK																	x
OR		x			x	x		x	x		x	x			x	x	
PA			x	x	x	x	x					x	x	x	x		
SC		x	x		x	x	x	x	x	x	x	x	x	x	x		
SD		x		x	x			x	x	x		x		x	x		
TX																	x
UT		x	x	x	x		x			x		x	x	x	x		
VT																	x

TABLE 8 *(continued)*
An Overview of Intervention Programs for
At-Risk Gifted Learners by State

	0 1	2	0 3	0 4	0 5	6	0 7	0 8	0 9	10	11	12	13	14	15	16	17
VA	x	x	x	x	x	x	x	x	x	x	x	x	x	x	x		
WA		x	x		x					x			x		x		
WV	x	x		x	x		x	x	x	x	x	x	x	x	x		
WI																x	
WY			x		x		x	x		x							

1 = Early Intervention
2 = Academic Programs
3 = Counseling
4 = Tutorials
5 = Mentorships
6 = Internships
7 = Arts Programs
8 = Creative Programs
9 = Academic Skill Development Emphasis
10 = Process Skill Development Programs
11 = Test Taking Skills
12 = Acceleration
13 = Nontraditional Placement
14 = Dual Enrollment Programs
15 = Independent Study
16 = Other
17 = NR
O = Program options clearly supported in the literature on at-risk students.

were used to some extent. Twenty-six programs (54.1%) indicated no or almost no differential programs or services addressed at-risk factors.

Very few districts responding showed congruence in their perspective about successes or problems in working with at-risk gifted students. At least two respondents perceived program successes to be: (a) achieving in the face of adversity, (b) the use of creative skills for personal and academic coping, (c) overcoming language difficulties, and (d) being identified for special programs. Problems were perceived to be in the following areas: (1) peer pressure, (2) a familial pattern often lacking resources that foster academic learning, (3) lack of self-esteem, (4) lack of funding for programs, (5) language differences and deficiencies, and (6) transiency.

TABLE 9
Approaches to Serving At-Risk
Gifted Students in Descending Order of Frequency

Programmatic Approach	Number	Percentage
Creative Programs	37	75.0
Process Skill Development	37	75.0
Academic Programs	36	72.9
Acceleration	29	56.3
Independent Study	23	45.8
Mentorships	22	43.8
Arts Programs	19	37.5
Academic Skill Development	18	35.4
Nontraditional Placements	15	29.2
Test Taking Skills	15	29.2
Early Interventions	14	27.1
Counseling Programs	13	24.1
Individual Tutorials	8	14.6
Other	5	10.4
Internships	3	6.3

Note: N = 51

Differential Characteristics of At-Risk Learners

Teacher perceptions about the characteristics that set at-risk gifted learners apart from more advantaged gifted learners are reported in Table 10. The pattern of responses is arranged in descending order of frequency. Teachers perceive affective insecurity, or the need for reassurance, as a variable that separates at-risk learners from other gifted children. Differences were also cited for the at-risk group in preference for oral expression.

At-risk students were perceived to be more erratic in their academic performance, with difficulty completing homework identified as a specific manifestation of the problem.

Curriculum and Instructional Factors

Districts responded on a 1-5 scale regarding their use of key curriculum tools that might address aspects in the background experience of at-risk gifted learners. More than 80% of the districts used the following approaches:

• Learning experiences representing a multi-cultural perspective.

TABLE 10
Number and Percentage of Programs Recognizing
Distinctive Characteristics Among At-Risk Learners

Characteristic	Number	Percentage
Preference for oral over written tasks	28	58.3
Need for confirmation of their abilities	28	58.3
Erratic academic performance	27	56.3
Need for frequent feedback on progress	24	50.0
Need for recognition for their accomplishments	20	41.7
Difficulty with homework completion	19	39.6
Preference for expressive activities	19	39.6
Daily reinforcement for their work	15	31.3
Procrastination over tasks	12	25.0
Flexibility in thinking patterns	10	20.8
Exhibit risk-taking behavior in classroom	8	16.7
Exhibit maturity	6	12.5
Quickness of warm-up	0	0

- Specific study of cultures represented by at-risk students.

- Use of biography to instill pride and identification with sex, race, and other background variables.

Almost half the programs, however, placed little emphasis on (1) parent awareness that focused on nurturing giftedness in the home, or (2) scholarship support for enrichment opportunities beyond the school.

When asked if special materials, handbooks, or guidelines had been developed by their state, 69.2% of the respondents (36) stated "no." Six states (11.5%) did not respond to this question. However, 19.2% (10) of the states indicated that these materials either exist or are being developed.

Only 10 districts reported they had developed special materials, handbooks, or guidelines for working with at-risk gifted learners, although seven districts indicated that work was in process.

Instructional Practices

Table 11 lists, in descending order, classroom strategies used in each district. The last column indicates the number of districts that employ a particular technique exclusively with at-risk gifted learners.

TABLE 11
Classroom Strategies Employed with
Gifted At-Risk Learners

Classroom Strategies	Total Use N	Differential Use with At-Risk Students N
Strong use of praise and encouragement	42	17
Verbal recognition of student ideas and feelings	41	19
Use of creative writing, role-playing	41	12
Parent participation	39	14
Concern for student learning style	37	18
Structured learning environments	35	13
Use of ethnic literature	35	13
Small adult-child ratio	34	10
Motivated principal and teacher's shared leadership	34	12
Use of diagnostic-prescriptive teaching	28	13
Emphasis on reading instruction	25	7
Direct service to families	12	8
Provisions for preschool experiences	10	2

Note: N = 51

PROGRAM EVALUATION

Forty-six percent (23) of the programs indicated that evaluation standards were the same for all gifted programs. Only 12% (6) indicated separate measures. When evaluation of program services was probed, only 32 districts responded. Table 12 lists techniques in descending order of use. Almost half the districts reporting (25) rated their evaluation process as very effective, (i.e., 4 or 5); 14 districts rated their evaluation as 2 or 3, indicating limited or moderate effectiveness. Nine districts did not provide data on this item. Only two of 57 districts reported that longitudinal follow-up data was available.

EFFECTIVE INTERVENTIONS WITH AT-RISK GIFTED LEARNERS

A good in-school program for at-risk students should provide rigorous course work, comparable to that provided to advantaged learners in the best school settings. Other school programs focus on remediating skill deficits or offer programs in nonacademic areas, such as the performing arts. Research on the effectiveness of such programs is meager. A few

TABLE 12
Percentage of Use of Evaluation Techniques
with Programs for At-Risk Gifted Students

Evaluation Technique	Number	Percentage of Use
Questionnaires to parents	25	52.1
Questionnaires to teachers	25	52.1
Product assessments	25	52.1
Questionnaires to students	21	43.8
Pre-post assessments	22	45.8
Process observation (checklist completed by teacher or outside evaluator)	19	39.6
Interviews	15	37.3
Longitudinal follow-up (2 years or more)	13	27.1
Case studies	4	8.3

Note: N = 32

programs provide counseling to families of at-risk learners on the route to developing their children's talent.

VanTassel-Baska and Chepko-Sade (1986) suggested some necessary initiatives for economically at-risk gifted learners, including:

1. Scholarship assistance for special lessons and programs during elementary and middle school.

2. Counseling programs for students and families, no later than middle school.

3. A peer tutoring model comprising older and younger at-risk gifted students to enhance role modeling and responsiveness to individual needs.

4. State and local policies and procedures that encourage early identification and appropriate program provisions.

5. Resources such as universities, community organizations, churches, laboratories, foundations, and so forth, to provide special programs and services.

Some of these ideas have been tried on a limited basis, but even where differential provisions have been initiated, there is no evidence of program effectiveness.

Successes have been recorded for economically at-risk and minority gifted learners in traditional gifted programs that employ common treatments across advantaged and at-risk populations (Baska, 1989). For example, the Chicago Public Schools Gifted Program serves 68% African-American students, over half of whom are low income. The Gary Community School District serves a 95% minority population, of whom 80% are low income.

Bruch (1978) reviewed the literature on culturally-different gifted children, concluded that there were many gaps, and stated that "no consistent plan for development of the culturally-different gifted has been encompassed to date" (p. 383). In 1990, there are relatively few studies on how at-risk gifted students are best served. One method of gaining insight into "what works" would be to broaden the concept, and examine effective strategies for educating at-risk students in general.

Early Intervention

Early intervention has been influential in reducing later incidence of academic problems for at-risk students (Ramey, Yeates, & Short, 1984; Seitz, Rosenbaum, & Apfel, 1985). Lazar (1981) reviewed studies that reported the progress of children in Head Start programs. He concluded that program participants were significantly more likely to complete high school, stay out of special education programs, and complete school careers without being retained. Similar findings were noted by Royce, Lazar, and Darlington (1983) in a study of children in preschool programs in the 1960s and 1970s. Lazar found the following were related to positive outcomes: "the earlier the better," low adult/child ratio, parent participation, and service to both the children and their families.

While it has been shown that early intervention is effective, this does not imply that later intervention is ineffective. Kagan (1976) reminds us that even when environmental factors slow development, the situation can be reversed if, "the environment after infancy is beneficial to growth" (p. 103).

Support for early intervention programs is generally viewed as the best policy initiative (National Committee for Economic Development, 1988). This position is confirmed in the literature (Brandt, 1986; Lazar, 1981; Schweinhart, 1985), but remains underutilized.

School Learning and Classroom Environment

How can schools provide a nurturing environment? Research on school and classroom environments is extensive. Much of this work focuses on schools with sizable populations of lower SES students (Lezotte & Bancroft, 1985; Mann, 1985; Maskowitz & Hayman, 1976; Ornstein, 1983; Sizemore, 1989; West, 1985). In an extensive review of the literature on educating at-risk learners, Ornstein (1983) cited several studies that showed the quality of school as an important factor in outcomes for these students. He listed leadership, supervision of teachers, teacher morale, emphasis on reading instruction, and communication with parents as influential factors. West (1985) found principal expectations and instructional support to be related to achievement in reading and mathematics in selected urban schools in New Jersey.

In her extensive work in the Pittsburgh Public Schools, Sizemore (1989) found that schools narrowed the achievement gap between Black and Caucasian learners when instructional leaders "set the tone for high expectations for achievement, accelerated growth, and high achievement in reading and mathematics." She noted that effective principals focused teachers, students, and parents on high achievement as their top priority. These principals could facilitate certain routine behaviors among teachers, students, and parents in pacing instruction and outcomes, monitoring and measuring student and school progress, evaluation, staff-development, discipline, and decision making. Her work reinforced several earlier studies that showed the strong, positive effect of high expectations, teacher sense of efficacy, and the use of clear, simple, and agreed upon rules for learning by at-risk students.

Comer's (1988) work in public schools has demonstrated the efficacy of teams of "caretakers" to bridge the sociocultural misalignment between schools and low SES home environments of culturally diverse students. The key to achievement, as viewed by Comer, is promotion of psychological, social, and intellectual development that encourages bonding to schools by fostering positive interactions among parents, students, and school personnel. The development of cohesive, involved, and empowered teams in the planning, implementation, supervision, and evolution of the total school program serves as a cornerstone to Comer's approach. Impressive increases in the academic and affective performance of low income culturally diverse students have resulted.

Murphy (1986) found structured learning environments, emphasis on mathematics and reading, staff development, parental involvement, and active, motivated leadership in schools that successfully teach at-risk students. Mann (1985) found that matching instruction to the child's learning style, and ensuring overlap between what is taught and what is tested, are important factors.

Maskowitz and Hayman (1976) studied style differences between "best" and first year teachers, primarily in lower SES junior-high classes, in a large northeastern city. The climate established by more successful teachers included greater use of: student ideas; praise and encouragement; verbal recognition of student feelings; time on task, and more activities per period.

Earlier, Hilliard (1976), and more recently Anderson (1989), noted the persistent mismatch between the cognitive styles of culturally diverse students, teaching style, and school environment. Anderson (1988) reported a debilitating effect on minority students when conflict occurs between their philosophical world views, conceptual systems, cognitive style, and the responses these different perspectives elicit from the education system. Their cognitive and behavior styles are often misconstrued by teachers and other educational personnel and, as noted by Anderson (1989), labeled as deficient. Shade (1978) observed that teachers often ostracize intellectually superior African-Americans because they do not "fit the stereotype."

Becker (1977) cited the importance of language development for at-risk learners. In Project Follow Through, he evaluated the progress of thousands of students in first to third grade and concluded, "Words are the building blocks of education. Teach the English language" (p. 542).

While language development is an obvious need in the early years, it is frequently replaced in junior- and senior-high by specialty-area curricula. Usova (1978) suggested techniques for motivating interest in reading with at-risk secondary students and included language-related methods, such as "acting out" reading material and reading aloud to students. Upward Bound, a program designed to help high school students prepare for college, emphasized language-based skills such as reading, composition, ethnic literature, and creative writing (Koe, 1980).

Traditionally, many low socioeconomic minority students have not taken advanced course work in mathematics and science. Anick, Carpenter, and Smith (1981) noted that serious inequities exist in the mathematics education of African-American and Hispanic-American students; that their achievement levels were well below the national average, and that differences from the larger population increased for each consecutive age group. Their study showed that African-Americans appear to take less mathematics than other groups, yet these students reported positive feelings about the subject. The authors concluded that motivation may not be a major problem, and that general approaches used for all students might be appropriate for minorities. Lincoln (1980) suggested the use of known objects in the environment as tools in teaching mathematics and science to these students.

After reviewing 9 years of research (24 studies) on participation and performance of minorities in mathematics, Mathews (1984) delineated parent, student, and school influences as important factors. She noted that although parents want to help their children, they often do not know how, that minority role models appear to have a positive effect on enrollment in mathematics courses, and that mathematics may be viewed by lower SES youngsters as lacking utility.

Counseling

The role of counseling in the education of at-risk learners has been somewhat controversial. Historically, many counselors have been unable to provide appropriate services because they did not understand the culture, cultural perspectives, and value systems of minority and low SES students. Therefore, counseling in schools is often viewed as ignoring cultural values or treating all students the same, despite cultural group membership. Some educators have argued that affective programming takes time away from cognitive instruction and expands the role of the school to encompass issues that are better dealt with by families. But if one views the child from a holistic perspective, the two are inseparable. Clearly, counselors can play a significant role in establishing closer relationships among the school, family, and community.

Researchers contend that school counseling prevents mental health problems (Pedro-Carroll, Cowen, Hightower, & Guare, 1986; Weissberg, Cowen, & Lotyczewski, 1983). Responses to problem solving and cognitive therapy techniques have been especially positive (Shure & Spivak, 1982; Kendall & Braswell, 1985).

Several authors noted specific techniques that enhanced counseling for at-risk learners. Griffith (1977) suggested that counselors can show respect for culturally diverse children by learning about their cultures; she also suggested that contact between minority youth and high-achieving minority adults should be facilitated. Exum (1983) cautioned that nonminority counselors need to be aware of various stages minority children may experience in adjusting to racism. Colangelo and Lafrenz (1981) urged counselors to be aware that minority children may experience peer pressure not to succeed. Smith (1981) suggested that counselors adopt a "sociotherapy" approach to counseling African-American learners. This approach encourages counselors to adopt multiple, comprehensive interventions that help individuals reach their potential in educational, social, and career development. She emphasized that counselors should focus on developing counseling goals and techniques that promote the positive individual and collective growth of the African-American (Smith, 1981).

Draper (1980) suggested that the following cultural norms may hinder the progress of minority students: (1) the degree of importance placed on social acceptance, (2) a tendency to reject solitary activity, and (3) sanctions against questioning cultural values. Colangelo and Exum (1979) postulate that culturally different students are likely to have different learning styles, suggesting that hands-on experiences and the gradual movement from a more structured to a less structured environment are appropriate classroom strategies. Researchers have also recommended mentors, community involvement, and early counseling that emphasizes future careers (Dunham & Russo, 1983). It must be noted that at-risk children within each group are different from one another; thus one cannot espouse a monolithic model for counseling these youngsters.

Mathematics and Science Programs

Nine local mathematics and science programs were found to be exemplary in educating highly able at-risk students (Alamprese, Erlanger & Brigham, 1988). Successful strategies used in these programs included:

- *The time students spend learning,* including after-school, weekend, and summer enrichment, and accelerated courses;

- *The operation of special programs* in the elementary grades that prepare students early for acceptance into highly selective gifted and talented programs;

- *The provision of accelerated courses* at local universities and programs offered by specialized schools in science and mathematics;

- *The use of hands-on learning techniques,* such as laboratory classes and independent research projects, to teach students how to apply mathematical and scientific concepts; and

- *The provision of out-of-school activities* designed to enhance students' cultural and intellectual development: museum programs, business and industry mentorship programs, and field trips.

The study also reported that the following affective strategies provided social emotional support:

- *External goals* that students can work toward, such as winning an academic contest or passing the Advanced Placement examination;

- *Career awareness programs* to inform students about the professional opportunities available in mathematics and science;

- *Social-emotional support* provided by teachers and counselors who are involved in students' lives; and

- *Encouragement of parent participation* in students' academic development and in supporting their emotional growth.

Figure 1 coalesces the research findings across several study areas on accepted strategies for intervention with at-risk learners. By synthesizing these findings across types of studies, we emerge with a clearer picture of generic interventions that appear to work well, given the nature of the population. These interventions include:

1. Early and systematic attention to the needs of these children.

2. Parental and family involvement in the educational program model.

3. Effective schools' strategies (e.g., time on task, principal leadership.)

4. Experiential and "hands-on" learning approaches.

5. Activities that allow for student self-expression.

6. Mentors and role models.

7. Community involvement.

8. Counseling efforts that address cultural values and facilitate talent development.

9. Building on the strengths and differential learning styles of at-risk learners.

The literature identifies general directions for intervention with the at-risk gifted learner. Practical application in school-based programs, however, remains elusive.

FIGURE 1
The At-Risk Student: A Chart of Research
Topics and Accepted Strategies for Intervention

Research Topics	Interventions
Early intervention	Preschool programs Small adult-child ratios Parent participation Service to families

School and classroom
  environment
	Motivated leadership/principal expectations
	Supervision of teachers
	High teacher morale
	Emphasis on reading instruction
	Communication with parents/parental
	  involvement
	Instructional support
	Structured, but flexible, learning environments
	Staff development
	Matching instruction to learning
	style/diagnostic-prescriptive teaching

Effective teachers	Use of student ideas Praise and encouragement Verbal recognition of student feelings Time on task High expectations for student performance More activities per period Sense of teacher efficacy
Language development	Teaching the English language Acting out what is read Use of ethnic literature Employ creative writing

Mathematics & Science	Use of familiar concrete objects as teaching
	  tools and hands-on learning techniques
	Use of minority role models
	Educating and involving parents
	Focusing on the value of math/science
	Extension of time through out-of-school
	  programs
	Provision of accelerated study through
	  universities and special schools
	Provision of career awareness programs

Counseling	Teach problem-solving strategies Use multiple approaches that include cognitive therapy techniques

FIGURE 1 *(continued)*
**The At-Risk Student: A Chart of Research
Topics and Accepted Strategies for Intervention**

Research Topics	Interventions
	Use mentors/role models
	Respect minority culture and related issues
	Exploration of cultural identity issue
	Focus on future career roles
	Early intervention
	Community involvement
Gifted "disadvantaged"	Use of mentors
	Community involvement
	Early counseling
	Hands-on learning experiences

SUMMARY

Programs for at-risk gifted learners must blend best practices gleaned from effective programs for all gifted learners with best practices that work with at-risk students in general. Labeling and creating stereotypes about at-risk students who fit the label must be avoided. Minority children may differ from one another in the degree to which they want to identify with or differentiate from their culture (Colangelo & Exum, 1979). Frasier (1979) reminds us that at-risk gifted students are not necessarily deprived of love or stimulation, nor deficient in specific thought processes or language. These students differ widely from one another, and programs must provide diverse opportunities to meet their needs. Cultural strengths and differences should be reflected in materials, curriculum, and when possible, personnel (Clasen, 1979). Programs must address the whole child and include basic life skills: problem solving, decision making, seeking assistance, discrimination of relevant and irrelevant information, and the development of self direction and control (Frasier, 1979). Programs must involve parents in the educational process, providing them with the knowledge, skills, and attitudes necessary to nurture their talented children.

While academic self-competence is not usually an issue for advantaged gifted learners, it may be a major concern for some at-risk students (VanTassel-Baska, Olszewski, & Kulieke, in press). In addition, some of these students, even those who perform well on typical in-grade standardized tests, do not score as well as their advantaged counterparts on more powerful test measures (VanTassel-Baska & Willis, 1987). Opportunities should be provided for counseling, mentorships, special tutorials, and other program options that promote and strengthen academic skills.

RECOMMENDATIONS

- Differential programming should be initiated as an additional level of service for all gifted students. Such programming should begin at the kindergarten level and focus on additional opportunities for:

  (1) Academic skill-building in reading, writing, mathematics, and science;

  (2) One-to-one mentorships or tutorials with older students or adults sharing similar characteristics;

  (3) Parent education and involvement in the learning process;

  (4) Encouragement and support in the regular learning environment through small group counseling.

- We must consider a nurturing environment as a critical variable in understanding the performance of students from differing socioeconomic and cultural groups. Evidence suggests that low socioeconomic status plays an important role in the tested achievement level of highly able students (VanTassel-Baska & Willis, 1987), and that cultural factors strongly influence cognition and behavior.

- We must examine the purpose of existing gifted programs and the related inferences about levels or types of intellectual functioning. For example, if a program requires students to engage in original production involving high level analytical and interpretive skills, then only students with these "readiness" skills should be exposed to such a challenging intervention. If, however, the program provides only mild enrichment, such as a special unit on archaeology with open-ended expectations, it is inappropriate to insist on high threshold scores for entry. As a field, we have not focused gifted programs well enough to justify the identification protocols used to select or eliminate students who would benefit from the program. Inconsistency between program definition and identification has made our identification processes vulnerable to being perceived as capricious or arbitrary.

5. Creative Problem-Solving in Finding Funds

The questionnaire sought to determine the level and type of funding used to encourage special programs for at-risk gifted students. The states were asked: (1) if funds were specifically allocated for program development, (2) the percentage of state and local contribution for statewide programs, (3) if other funds were available, and (4) if funding sources were "set aside" for state educational agencies.

Data from the 52 states and territories reveal that little attention is given to proportional funding for special populations of gifted students. Only one state reported that funds were specifically allocated to programs for at-risk gifted learners. The lack of proportional funding can be attributed to two factors: (1) total state budgets for all gifted programs are somewhat small; and (2) efforts to conduct research and development on underrepresented populations have just begun.

A variety of approaches is used to encourage funding. Only one of 47 states (2.4%) uses "set asides" and "identification standards." "Documentation in the State Plan" is used by 12.8% of the states. "Goals for disadvantaged participation" were reported by 19% of the states. Twelve states (36.7%) indicated "other approaches" were used to encourage funding. Table 13 reflects the percent of use of the various approaches to state funding.

Forty-three respondents (91%) do not allocate state funds for at-risk gifted programs. Two states did not respond to the question. Three states (5.8%) indicated that 50% of their funds originated at the state level. Six respondents indicated differing percentages of state funding, ranging from 62% to 99%.

TABLE 13
State Approaches to Encourage Funding for
At-Risk Gifted Students

Approaches	Frequency	Percentage
Set Asides	1	2.1
Goals for "Disadvantaged" Participation	9	19.0
Documentation in the State Plan	6	12.8
Identification Standards	1	1.9
Other Approaches	12	36.7

Note: N = 52

Forty-four states (84.6%) did not respond to the question on local contributions allocated for special programs for at-risk gifted. The remaining states
(15.4%) indicated differing percentages of local funding allocations,
ranging from 6% to 99% of the local contributions for funding programs
for gifted students.

One state indicated that 20% of their funds were specifically desig-
nated for at-risk gifted students. Only 2 states responded to this question.

The most recent delineation of total state funds allocated to programs
for gifted students was compiled by the National Association of State
Directors of Gifted Programs (Houseman, 1987). States responding to the
survey revealed interesting data regarding both increases and decreases in
state funding. Figure 2 depicts the general level of support by state. In
addition, Figure 2 provides a state-by-state breakdown of funds distributed
to local education agencies for gifted and talented programs.

FIGURE 2
State Appropriations for Education of Gifted Students (adapted from
the 1987 Council of State Director's State of the State Report).

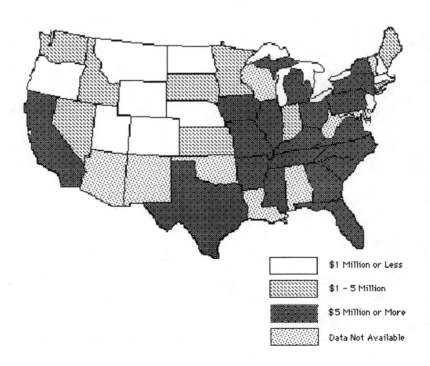

Given the fluctuations of funding for the gifted in many states over the past three years, it is understandable that state and local personnel have not systematically addressed the issue of program funding for at-risk gifted students.

FEDERAL FUNDING INITIATIVES

In *A Nation At Risk* (1983), The National Commission on Excellence in Education said, "The Federal Government, in cooperation with states and localities, should help meet the needs of key groups of students such as the gifted and talented" (p. 32).

Until recently however, lack of federal involvement has placed the total burden of support and monitoring on states and localities. Since the states varied widely in terms of interest or ability to assist localities in the development and maintenance of gifted programs in general, the plight of special populations of gifted learners had been bleak.

Four years after *A Nation At Risk*, Congress passed the first federal initiative to aid education for gifted and talented students. This meager $20 million authorization, included in a larger Omnibus Education Bill, provided funds for research, personnel preparation, and innovative projects. The Javits Gifted and Talented Students Education Act of 1988 appropriated an initial $20 million to provide for a National Research Center and model projects that focus on at-risk gifted learners.

RECOMMENDATIONS

- States and local districts need to consider set-aside funding for at-risk gifted learners. Collaborative efforts on this issue with sources such as Title I, migrant education, and various ethnic coalitions should be undertaken.

- At-risk students should receive priority for special funding obtained from outside sources (foundations, businesses, PTAs) that will provide extra programs during their first years of schooling.

SUMMARY

If progress is to be made in providing for more at-risk gifted students, we should be concerned about the results of this study. The data reflected limited concern for the special circumstances and needs of at-risk gifted students. This situation should be viewed with some concern for the following reasons:

1. Society is becoming more pluralistic. Projections of population growth by the year 2000 indicate a doubling of school-age minority students.

2. Society reflects a greater percentage of poor children than ten years ago. Projections for the future predict dramatic increases.

3. The increasing number of single parent families headed by women (particularly African-Americans), coupled with low income, increases the risk for many at-risk gifted students.

These demographic trends reflect the need for greater attention to this population by the field of gifted education. To have significant impact, the field must unify around a common understanding of whom the at-risk learners are, how they can be identified, and the interventions that are most important for them to receive. Since gifted education cannot solve these problems alone, we must reach out to other sections of the educational community for assistance.

New federal initiatives in this area must find a way to impact on states, since the states influence development of local programs and services for the at-risk gifted population. As data in this study suggest, however, a focus on the at-risk gifted student is not, with a few notable exceptions, a major priority in the state framework. If we wish to enhance efforts in this area, state policy makers must be made more aware of the issues and be encouraged to incorporate them into state standards and funding formulas.

6. Suggestions for a Working Agenda

Eliminate the use of the term "disadvantaged." The use of the term "disadvantaged" in describing culturally diverse populations carries a negative value connotation. Cultures differ normatively from each other; inherently, no one culture or class of individuals is superior to another. The term "cultural diversity" acknowledges their identity without assigning a value judgment.

Professionals have often resorted to negative terminology to promote awareness of inequities in our educational system. "Disadvantaged," like the word "handicapped," carries both a negative connotation and a generic notion of deficit or deficiency. This notion is problematic because individuals can be both economically disadvantaged and resilient, handicapped and gifted. Because the term is so generic, it frequently creates its own meaning in a particular local context.

To identify children who may be at-risk for educational opportunities commensurate with their abilities as "disadvantaged" is to diffuse the issue in a way that blocks appropriate interventions. It is much more appropriate to consider the factors that contribute to at-risk status—low socioeconomic status, membership in an ethnic or racial group, a specific disability, a consistently unstable home environment (e.g., alcoholism, abuse), or limited proficiency in English. These factors should be viewed as the basis for special identification and intervention approaches, whether they are present in 1% or 80% of a given school district population. In contexts where both "at-risk" and "at-promise" conditions prevail, educators of the gifted are obliged to intervene.

The terms "unserved" and "underserved" have also been used to describe this population. These terms further confuse the issue. There are many other subpopulations of gifted learners who remain unserved or underserved—the highly gifted, gifted women, young primary gifted children, and certain categories of giftedness like leadership. Factors that place a developing child at risk for appropriate educational attention, including sociological, educational, and political issues, are more useful for formulating policy.

Translate expressed philosophical concerns for "at-risk" learners into definitional structures of giftedness. All levels of data collection have a strong orientation toward including at-risk learners in gifted programs. Yet, at the point of entry into the program structure, few states and local districts develop an inclusive statement for their operational definitions (Patton, VanTassel-Baska, & Prillaman, 1990; VanTassel-Baska, Patton, & Prillaman, 1989). It is as if rhetoric is expected to carry over into policy without deliberately planning for it. Until educational institutions explicitly define who they are talking about when they refer to at-risk gifted learners and seek to identify and program for them, the status of service will show little change.

An example of a definitional structure that focuses on explicit groups follows:

1. Students who come from low income families in which the parents' educational level and occupational status is also commensurately low.

2. Students who come from different cultural and racial backgrounds, and require an understanding of their cultural perspective to find and serve them appropriately.

3. Students who possess limited English proficiency due to recency of immigration or community norms.

4. Students who possess physical or learning disabilities that mask their potential.

5. Students who come from dysfunctional family backgrounds (children who are abused, children from alcoholic families, etc.).

6. Students who possess a combination of these characteristics.

Initiate the use of multiple measures, including assessment measures perceived to be approaching cultural and racial fairness for the identification and selection of at-risk students into gifted programs. If our goal is to find promising at-risk learners, we must find ways to establish a pool of such students within each risk factor category. Such a task calls for nontraditional approaches. Key factors to consider in developing identification protocols for at-risk learners include:

• Use of a mixture of objective and subjective assessment tools;

• Use of multiple criteria assessment measures and flexible program cut-off points on assessment measures;

• Use of nontraditional tests and other measures that tap diverse talent areas;

• Use of assessment data as a tool for planning curriculum

We must maintain a logical consistency in our procedures for identifying at-risk gifted learners. If we are willing to entertain both a multiple criteria model of identification and a quota system, then we should be equally willing to entertain the idea of multiple program options based on aptitude and interest. If we accept the premise that populations of gifted students have different characteristics and needs, then we must accept the premise that some differential programming will be required to meet these needs. This brings us to the question, "What program interventions are most needed by at-risk gifted students and what are the implications of meeting their individual needs?" Should the focus of these programs be academically different than those for advantaged students, or more creative and open-ended than for other groups of gifted learners? We also need to decide if all gifted students should be immersed in a multifaceted set of program opportunities that allows for wide deviations among individual profiles. These philosophical and program issues are far more encompassing than identification, and represent critical areas worthy of closer scrutiny. If we broaden identification criteria to include more at-risk students, then funnel them into a narrow conception of gifted program designs, we do them the ultimate disservice by attaching a label that conveys the opposite impression from the students' real program experiences.

Recognize and address the special education needs of at-risk gifted learners who share many commonalities with all gifted learners, but may vary in significant ways. To meet the needs of at-risk gifted learners, educators must combine unique elements used in defining, identifying, and developing programs for these learners with qualitatively different approaches needed for all gifted learners. Just as gifted children share common characteristics with all learners, at-risk gifted learners share many characteristics with both typical learners and other gifted learners.

We need to examine our fundamental purpose for implementing gifted programs, our capacity to manage individual and group differences and needs, and our willingness to operate multiple program options and to define reasonable student outcomes. Only after responding to these concerns can we do justice to this special population of learners.

Our efforts to program, however, must focus also in the area of difference from traditionally identified gifted learners. Special characteristics create special educational needs that should be addressed differentially if we are to enhance the capacities of at-risk students. For example, a child from a single-parent family may need special counseling assistance; a low-income child may need scholarship assistance for special lessons or programs; a child whose family has recently immigrated to the United States may need opportunities to meet regularly with other recent immigrants. A recognition of diversity and a willingness to address these factors are required in charting a qualitatively distinctive program.

Encourage the use of a "tryout" program for all students nominated to the gifted program in which responsiveness to differentiated classroom curriculum becomes a part of the selection paradigm. Too many methods for gifted student identification are developed in a vacuum, without any relationship to the actual curriculum provided. This situation is especially problematic when we consider at-risk students who are overlooked in our quest to find the traditionally gifted learner. We need to reverse the order of program development so that enriched opportunities in the classroom become one level of identification. We shall then have established an important, yet frequently missing, link between identification and curriculum intervention.

Develop program prototypes for use with atypical gifted learners. A need exists for prototypes for intervention with at-risk gifted learners. Many interventions use the equal-treatment model as the standard for all gifted programs. Providing equal-treatment has merit, but there is greater merit in different or additional levels of programming that address the unique needs of at-risk students. This differentiated, value-added programming might be offered in the context of the regular gifted program through an Individualized Education Plan (IEP) model, individual contract, or more personalized delivery of services. Special groupings of learners based on a particular risk factor might have merit.

Develop individual services such as tutoring, mentoring, and counseling for at-risk gifted learners. Insight into what works for at-risk learners suggests the importance of personalized services, delivered by caring individuals who understand the nature of the child's culture and socioeconomic status, and can help him or her negotiate education successfully. Such individuals represent important links for at-risk learners in the schools. Volunteer assistance may be necessary to provide the level of personalized service these learners require. Two groups of volunteers should be considered: (a) highly skilled retirees and women who are not in the work force, and (b) college or high school students who might work in such a program as a community service contribution. It is important to ensure a match between the helpers and the students to be served. The matching process should consider cultural background, gender, and SES level. If businesses want to assist, a community support network for these learners could be a significant contribution.

Consider a "matching funds" model to encourage program development for at-risk gifted students. Funding models will need to go beyond the regular gifted budget to provide viable programs and services. A focus on each at-risk factor seems the best strategy, with emphasis on factors with the highest incidence rate. Shared funding provides the flexibility to try new practices and prototypes. Unless additional incentive funding is obtained, the current level of limited programming is likely to prevail.

Collect systematic data on at-risk students served in gifted programs. The success of work with at-risk learners depends on long-term collection and evaluation of data about program practices, and the impact of effective programs on students' lives. Since the evaluation problem is endemic of the field of gifted education in general, it may be difficult to accomplish this needed program measure, but important enough to improve practices in this regard.

References

Alamprese, J. A., & Erlanger, W. J. , & Brigham, N. (1988). *No gift wasted: Effective strategies for educating highly able, disadvantaged students in mathematics and science* (Vols. 1-2). USOE contract #300-87-0152. Washington, DC: United States Department of Education.

Anderson, J. A. (1988). Theme: Minorities—cognitive styles and multicultural populations. *Journal of Teacher Education, 39*(1), 2-9.

Anderson, J. A. (1989). Cognitive styles and multicultural populations. *Journal of Teacher Education, 39*(1), 2-9.

Anick, C. M., Carpenter, T. P., & Smith, C. (1981). Minorities and mathematics: Results from the national assessment of educational progress. *Mathematics Teacher, 74*(7), 560-566.

Baldwin, A. Y. (1985). Programs for the gifted and talented. Issues concerning minority populations. In F. D. Horowitz and M. O'Brien (Eds.), *The gifted and talented: Developmental perspectives* (pp. 223-249). Washington, DC: American Psychological Association.

Baldwin, A. Y. (1987). I'm Black but look at me, I am also gifted. *Gifted Child Quarterly, 31,* 180-85.

Baska, L. (1989). Are current identification protocols unfair to the minority disadvantaged student? In C. J. Maker (Ed.) *Critical issues in gifted education* (pp. 226-236). Rockville, MD: Aspen Publications.

Becker, W. C. (1977). Teaching reading and language to the disadvantaged: What we have learned from field research. *Harvard Educational Review, 47*(4), 518-543.

Bernal, E. M., & Reyna, J. (1974). Analysis of giftedness in Mexican-American children and design of a prototype instrument. Report for Southwest Educational Development Lab, Austin, TX. Office of Education (DHEW). Contract #4-7-062113-307. Washington, DC: Office for Gifted and Talented.

Brandt, R. (1986). On long-term effects of early education: A conversation with Lawrence Schweinhart. *Educational Leadership, 44*(3), 14-18.

Bruch, C. B. (1975). Assessment of creativity in culturally different gifted children. *Gifted Child Quarterly, 19*(2), 164-174.

Bruch, C. B. (1978). Recent insights on the culturally different gifted. *Gifted Child Quarterly, 22*(3), 374-393.

Clasen, R. E. (1979). Models for the educational needs of gifted children in a multicultural context. *Journal of Negro Education, 48,* 357-363.

Colangelo, N., & Exum, H. A. (1979). Educating the culturally diverse gifted: Implications for teachers, counselors and parents. *Gifted Child Today, 6,* 23-24 and 54-55.

Colangelo, N., & Lafrenz, N. (1981). Counseling the culturally diverse gifted. *Gifted Child Quarterly, 25,* 27-30.

Comer, J. (1988). Educating poor minority children. *Scientific American, 259*(5), 42-47.

Draper, W. (1980, Fall). The creative and gifted minority student: Interviews with Ambrocio Lopez and Charles Payne. *Creative Child and Adult Quarterly, 5*(3), 171-179.

Dunham, G., & Russo, T. (1983). Career education for the disadvantaged gifted: Some thoughts for educators. *Roeper Review, 5*(3), 26-28.

Exum, H. H. (1983). Key issues in family counseling with gifted and talented Black students. *Roeper Review, 5*(3), 28-31.

Feldman, D. (1983). *Developmental conceptions of giftedness.* San Francisco, CA: Jossey Bass.

Feuerstein, R. (1979). *The dynamic assessment of retarded performers: The learning potential assessment device, theory, instruments and techniques.* Baltimore, MD: University Park Press.

Frasier, M. (1989). Identification of gifted Black students: Developing new perspectives. In J. Maker (Ed.), *Critical issues in gifted education, Volume II,* (pp. 213-225). Rockville, MD: Aspen Publications.

Frasier, M. M. (1979). Rethinking the issue regarding the culturally disadvantaged gifted. *Exceptional Children, 45*(7), 538-542.

Gardner, H. (1983). *Frames of mind.* New York: Basic Books.

Gay, J. (1978). A proposed plan for identifying Black gifted children. *Gifted Child Quarterly, 22*(3), 353-360.

Griffith, A. R. (1977). A cultural perspective for counseling Blacks. *Humanist Educator, 16*(2), 80-85.

Hilliard, A. (1976). *Alternative to IQ testing: An approach to the identification of the gifted in minority children* (Report No. 75175). San Francisco, CA: San Francisco State University.

Houseman, W. (1987). *The 1987 state of the states gifted and talented report.* Topeka, KS: The Council of State Directors of Programs for the Gifted.

Jencks, C. (1972). *Inequality.* New York: Basic Books.

Kagan, J. (1976). Resilience and continuity in psychological development. In A. M. Clarke and A. D. B. Clarke (Eds.), *Early experience: Myth and evidence* (pp. 97-121). New York: The Free Press.

Kendall, P. C., & Braswell, L. (1985). *Cognitive behavior therapy with impulsive children.* New York: The Guilford Press.

Koe, F. T. (1980). Supplementing the language instruction of the culturally different learner: Upward bound program. *English Journal, 69,* 19-20.

Lazar, I. (1981). Early intervention is effective. *Educational Leadership, 38,* 303-305.

Lezotte, L. W., & Bancroft, B. A. (1985). School improvement based on effective schools research: A promising approach for economically disadvantaged and minority students. *Journal of Negro Education, 54*(3), 301-311.

Lincoln, E. (1980). Tools for teaching math and science students in the inner city. *School Science and Math, 80,* 3-7.

Mann, D. (1985). Effective schools for children of the poor. *Education Digest, 51,* 24-25.

Marland, S. (1972). *U. S. report to congress on the gifted and talented.* Washington, DC: Government Printing Office.

Maskowitz, G., & Hayman, J. T. (1976). Success strategies of inner city teachers: A year-long study. *Journal of Educational Research, 69,* 283-289.

Mathews, W. (1984). Influences on the learning and participation of minorities in math. *Journal for Research in Math Education, 15*(2), 84-95.

McClelland, D. C. (1978). Managing motivation to expand human freedom. *American Psychologist, 33,* 201-210.

Miller, L. (1974). *The testing of Black students: A symposium.* Englewood Cliffs, NJ: Prentice-Hall.

Minnesota State Department of Education (1987). *Guidelines for program development for gifted students.* St. Paul, MN: Author.

Moore, B. (1978). Career education for disadvantaged gifted high school students. *Gifted Child Quarterly, 22*(3), 332-337.

Murphy, D. M. (1986). Educational disadvantagement. *Journal of Negro Education, 55*(4), 495-507.

National Committee for Economic Development (1988). *Children in need.* Washington, DC.

National Committee on Excellence in Education (1983). *A nation at risk: The imperative for educational reform.* Washington, DC: United States Department of Education.

Nebraska State Department of Education (1986). *Regulations for establishing programs for gifted and talented.* Lincoln, NE: Author.

Olszewski, P., Kulieke, M., Willis, G., & Krasney, N. (1987). *A study of the predictors of success in fast paced classes and the validity of entrance scores.* Evanston, IL: Northwestern University, Center for Talent Development.

Ornstein, A. C. (1983). Educating disadvantaged learners. *Educational Forum, 47*(2), 225-247.

Patton, J. M., VanTassel-Baska, J., & Prillaman, D. (1990). The nature and extent of programs for the disadvantaged gifted in the United States and territories. *Gifted Child Quarterly, 34*(3), 94-96.

Pedro-Carroll, J. L., Cowen, E. L., Hightower, D. A., & Guare, J. C. (1986). Preventive intervention with latency-aged children of divorce: A replication study. *American Journal of Community Psychology, 14*(3), 277-290.

Ramey, C. T., Yeates, K. O., & Short, E. J. (1984). The plasticity of intellectual development: Insights from preventive intervention. *Child Development, 55,* 1913-1925.

Renzulli, J. (1978). What makes giftedness: Re-examining a definition. *Phi Delta Kappan, 60,* 180-184.

Renzulli, J., Smith, L., White, A., Callahan, C., & Hartman, R. (1976). *Scales for rating behavioral characteristics of superior students.* Mansfield Center, CT: Creative Learning Press.

Royce, J., Lazar, I., & Darlington, R. B. (1983). Minority families, early education, and later life chances. *American Journal of Orthopsychiatry, 53*(4), 706-720.

Samuda, R. J. (1975). *Psychological testing of American minorities: Issues and consequences.* New York: Dodd, Mead and Co.

Schweinhart, L. J. (1985). *The preschool challenge. High/scope early childhood policy papers, no. 4.* Ypsilanti, MI: High/Scope Education Research Foundation.

Sears, P., & Sears, R. (1980). 1528 little geniuses and how they grew. *Psychology Today,* February, 28-43.

Seitz, V., Rosenbaum, L. K., & Apfel, N. H. (1985). Effects of family support intervention: A ten-year follow-up. *Child Development, 56,* 376-391.

Shade, B. (1978). Social-psychological traits of achieving Black children. *The Negro Educational Review, 19*, 80-86.

Shure, M. B., & Spivak, G. (1982). Interpersonal problem-solving in young children: A cognitive approach to prevention. *American Journal of Community Psychology, 10*(3), 341-356.

Sizemore, B. (1989). The algebra of African-American achievement. In *Effective schools: Critical issues in the education of Black children* (pp.124-149). Washington, DC: National Alliance of Black School Educators.

Smith, E. J. (1981). Cultural and historical perspectives in counseling Blacks. In *Counseling the culturally different: Theory and practice* (pp. 141-185). New York: John Wiley and Sons.

Sternberg, R. (1985). *Beyond IQ: A triarchic theory of human intelligence.* Cambridge: Cambridge University Press.

Torrance , E. P. (1969). Creative positives of disadvantaged children and youth. *Gifted Child Quarterly, 13*, 71-81.

Torrance, E. P. (1971). Are the Torrance Tests of Creative Thinking biased against or in favor of disadvantaged groups? *Gifted Child Quarterly, 15*, 75-80.

Torrance, E. P. (1977). *Discovery and nurturance of giftedness in the culturally different.* Reston, VA: The Council for Exceptional Children.

United States Bureau of the Census. 1986. *Statistical Abstract of the United States: 1987* (107th edition). Washington, DC: U.S. Government Printing Office.

United States Department of Commerce, Bureau of the Census. 1980. *Definition of poverty and poverty thresholds.* Washington, DC: U.S. Government Printing Office.

United States Department of Labor, Bureau of Labor Statistics. 1984. *Four-region classification system.* Washington, DC: U. S. Government Printing Office.

Usova, G. (1978). Techniques for motivating interest in reading for the disadvantaged high school student. *Reading, 15*(1), 36-38.

VanTassel-Baska, J., & Chepko-Sade, D. (1986). *An incidence study of disadvantaged gifted students in the midwest.* Evanston, IL: Center for Talent Development, Northwestern University.

VanTassel-Baska, J., Olszewski, P., & Kulieke, M. (in press). Differences among special populations of gifted learners on intra-personal dimensions.

VanTassel-Baska, J., Patton, J., & Prillaman, D. (1989). A national survey of programs and practices for at risk learners. *Focus on Exceptional Children, 22*(3), 1-15.

VanTassel-Baska, J., & Willis, G. (1987). A three-year study of the effects of low income on SAT scores among the academically able. *Gifted Child Quarterly, 31*, 169-173.

Weissberg, R. P., Cowen, E. L., & Lotyczewski, B. S. (1983). The primary health project: Seven consecutive years of program outcome research. *Journal of Consulting and Clinical Psychology, 51*(1), 100-107.

West, C. (1985). Effects of school climate and school social structure on student academic achievement in selected urban elementary schools. *Journal of Negro Education, 54*(3), 451-461.

Witty, E. P. (1978). Equal educational opportunity for gifted minority children. *Gifted Child Quarterly, 22*(3), 344-352.

APPENDICES

Program Abstracts

State Questionnaire

Local School District Questionnaire

Note: Program abstracts are based on information received from local school district personnel, not from on-site observations by the authors.

Program Abstracts

Program Title
Gifted Program

Purpose/Goals
1. To extend performance in verbal and quantitative reasoning;
2. To broaden intellectual and creative abilities with an emphasis on self-direction;
3. To increase problem-solving skills and inquiry techniques;
4. To provide exposure in career opportunities;
5. To broaden the development of research skills and research methods.

Population
Grades K-8. Sixty-nine percent of the student population is Hispanic, Native American, Black, or Asian.

Description
Assessment: Screening is by teacher, parent, and student referral, and achievement test scores. Placement is by several cognitive measures.

Service Delivery: The model used is a combination of the Autonomous Learner Model (George Betts and Jolene Knapp), the Renzulli Program Model, and the approach of Hilda Taba. Regular classroom instruction with clustering and pullout are used in grades 3 through 8 with a certified teacher of the gifted. In grades K and 1, the teacher of the gifted serves a consultant role to the regular class teacher. Identified students have an Individualized Educational Plan and semester and annual reviews.

Contact and Address
Robert A. Shaw, Director Special and Compensatory Education
Laveen Elementary Dist. No. 59
P. O. Box 29
Laveen, AZ 85339-0029
602/257-4972

Program Title
Discovery

Purpose/Goals
Delivery of flexible services to gifted and talented students based on individual, small group, and overall district strengths and needs. Stressed are:

1. Educator identification of students rather than traditional achievement testing;
2. Resources spent on services rather than screening;
3. Integration of school-based and community-based resources; and
4. Integration of gifted/talented programming into regular education in struction.

Population
Grades P-12.

Description
Assessment: Identification through educator nomination.

Service Delivery: The program provides quarterly exploratories in the arts and sciences, field trips, individual and group acceleration, regular classroom enrichment, and summer and after-school programs.

Student Outcomes: There have been increases in the number of minority students identified and successfully served through Discovery.

Transition: Opportunities for development of talent and academic skills are articulated for the purpose of higher level coursework at the middle school and ultimately high school levels.

Follow-up: Individual and group evaluation to access skills and opportunities/participation by minority and at-risk students.

Contact and Address
Peggy Reynolds, Discovery Coordinator
Fort Lupton School District RE 8
301 Reynolds Street
Fort Lupton, CO 80621

Program Title
Encendiendo Una Llama

Purpose/Goals
Identification and instruction of limited-English-proficient gifted and talented students.

Population
Grades K-6. Limited-English-proficient (LEP) children in schools in which they comprise over 60% of students.

Description
Assessment: Students are identified through a 3-step process:

1. Open recruitment (referrals, parental recommendation, test scores, and recognized achievement);
2. Talent pool membership in which students (about 10-15%) of school population participate on a trial basis in program services; and
3. Formal identification (based on the trial participation, supportive test data, and a cumulative record review).

During this process, individual student strengths, needs, and interest areas are assessed and an Individual Educational Program (IEP) is developed.

Service Delivery: All instruction is modeled on "Enrichment Triad" concepts developed by J. Renzulli. The program model has three components:

1. Resource room and full time bilingual resource teacher with instructional activities on a "pull-out" basis emphasizing small group instruction and independent projects;
2. After school program, taught by regular class teachers in their areas of expertise; provide instructional activities in such areas as science, language, computers, or art;
3. Regular class component in which students receive accelerated and/or enriched instruction.

Student Outcomes: In operation since 1979, the program has identified and served over 1,000 students.

Contact and Address
Dr. Gerald Gorman, Coordinator Gifted Programs
Bilingual Gifted and Talented Program
Webster School, 5 Cone St.
Hartford, CT 06105
203/722-8931

Program Title
Minority Excellence Program in Science

Purpose/Goals
Provision of enrichment activities to enhance program participants' self-concept, awareness of power to excel, and sense of community.

Population
High school minority students.

Description
Student Outcomes: A higher high school graduation rate for project minority students than for nonproject students. Increased representation of project minority students on the honor rolls.

Follow-up: Twenty-one graduates of the program are presently enrolled in institutions of higher education.

Contact and Address
Joe L. Beard, Program Coordinator
Gifted Program, Chicago Public Schools
Alton Board of Education
1854 E. Broadway
Alton, IL 62002-6664

Program Title
Chicago Gifted Program

Purpose/Goals
The proposed program will use multiple criteria for gifted identification and service delivery.

Population
Limited-English-proficient (LEP) Hispanic gifted students in grades 7 and 8.

Description
Assessment: Nomination and application forms will be in Spanish. A matrix approach will allow several combinations of scores for determining student eligibility. Raven's Progressive Matrices will also be used to minimize cultural bias.

Service Delivery: Proposes use of the "off-campus" model utilizing local museums and universities to provide school year and summer programs. The program is to be taught in Spanish by bilingual teachers or staff members at the institutions.

Contact and Address
Sue Maxwell, Project Director
Board of Education
Gifted Program Office
6 Center South/West
1819 W. Pershing Rd.
Chicago, IL 60609
312/535-8325 or 535-8324

Program Title
Rockford Gifted Program: Identification and Programming for Minority, Disadvantaged, and Limited-English-Proficient Gifted Learners.

Purpose/Goals
Provision of a differentiated approach to identification and program services for this specific population.

Population
Minority, disadvantaged, and limited-English-proficient (LEP) students in ten elementary schools within economically disadvantaged neighborhoods. Currently serves grades 1 to 3.

Description
Assessment: The Stanford Early School Achievement Test (SESAT) is administered at the end of the first semester of the kindergarten year. Top students and additional students identified through teacher referral were further tested with the Test of Non-Verbal Intelligence (TONI) during the first program year and the Raven Colored Progressive Matrices Test (CPM) the second year. Final identification is by matrix analysis of test scores and teacher input.

Service Delivery: The program provides self-contained classes within the students' neighborhood. It focuses on:
1. Specific curricular intervention through intellectual and grade/age level interaction; and
2. Provision of an affective support system.

The basic curriculum parallels the standard gifted curriculum in the District and includes a problem-solving approach to mathematics, a specific children's literature program, thinking skills instruction, creative thinking, hands-on science units, and frequent field trips.

Contact and Address
Gary E. Heidemam, Gifted Program Office
201 South Madison St.
Rockford, IL 61108
815/966-3182

Program Title
TOP: TAG Opportunity Program

Purpose/Goals
Identification and service delivery to potentially gifted minority students at the high school level. The program is designed to promote high academic achievement while addressing other components of giftedness including leadership, self-expression, and creativity.

Population
High school students who have language patterns and experience, cultural backgrounds, economic, and/or educational disadvantages or differences which make it difficult for them to demonstrate their potential on traditional identification measures.

Description
Assessment: The program uses a checklist of observable behavior characteristics of the minority gifted. It also uses the Structure of Intellect Learning Abilities Test.

Service Delivery: Features include:
1. Activities to stimulate thinking skills, communication skills, and research skills;
2. Concentration on cooperative learning strategies;
3. Off-site experiences and guest presentations;
4. Team teaching;
5. Class size not to exceed 25 students;
6. Uniform requirements;
7. Recognition incentives to increase student motivation; and
8. Regular school-home communication.

Contact and Address
David L. Smith
Prince George's County Public Schools
Upper Marlboro, MD 20772-9983

Program Title
Project STEP: Strategies for Targeting Early Potential

Purpose/Goals
Identification and nurturance of potentially gifted minority children in kindergarten and first grade for possible inclusion into the Talented and Gifted Program.

Population
K-1 potentially gifted minority children.

Description
Assessment: The program uses checklists, tasks, and other activities designed to aid teacher observation and recording of specific behaviors associated with giftedness, but not demonstrable in a formal test situation.

Contact and Address
David L. Smith
Prince George's County Public Schools
Upper Marlboro, MD 20772-9983

Program Title
Community Based Education (CBE) Program for Disadvantaged and Minority Student Achievement

Purpose/Goals
Identification and provision of enrichment services for minority children. Emphasis is on:
1. Higher order thinking strategies;
2. Problem solving, decision making, and creative thinking instructional contexts;
3. Accommodation to learning styles; and
4. Development of self-esteem.

Population
Minority and disadvantaged children in grades K-3 who are high-achieving children, but who do not qualify for the Academically Talented Program because of poor test performance.

Description
Assessment: Minority students who perform in top 20-25%, but do not qualify for the Academically Talented Program because of poor test performance are identified.

Service Delivery: Inquiry or guided discovery in a problem-solving context model is provided in community locations including churches and a community meeting room. Instructional methodology includes hands-on and experiential opportunities and de-emphasizes paper/pencil tasks.

Student Outcomes: After one year 80% of students qualified for the regular Academically Talented Program.

Transition: Students may move into the District's Academically Talented Program.

Follow-up: Students who enter the Academically Talented Program are invited back to CBE for support services.

Contact and Address
Jean Schmeichel, Specialist Academically Talented Programs
Department of Elementary Education, Academically Talented Program
Kalamazoo Public Schools
1220 Howard St.
Kalamazoo, MI 49008
616/384-0148

Program Title
Flint Community Schools' Magnet Programs, Gifted and Talented Magnet Program.

Purpose/Goals
Provision of multiple programs concentrating on particular subjects, interest areas, or teaching styles at elementary, middle, and senior-high schools to meet individual student talents and needs.

Population
Grades K-12. The G/T magnet program serves grades K-6.

Description
Service Delivery: Provides a differentiated curriculum model developed by J. Renzulli which comprises four components:
1. Basic curriculum in which students advance based on their achievement;
2. Type I exploratory enrichment activities;
3. Type II process skills: instructional activities to develop high-level thinking and feeling skills;
4. Type III product activities in which students investigate real problems or topics of their choice.

Contact and Address
Nona Gibbs , Coordinator
Human Resources and Magnet Programs
Magnet Program Office
923 E. Kearsley Street
Flint, MI 48202
313/762-1209

Program Title
Gifted and Talented Program, Hardin Public Schools

Population
Gifted students in grades K-12 of which about 50% are Native American.

Description
Assessment: The instrument used for measuring intellectual ability, the Kaufman Assessment Battery for Children (K-ABC), is not language- or achievement-centered, and has been found through local research to be culture-fair and appropriate for use with Native American children.

Service Delivery: Special efforts are made to include Native American cultural activities in the G/T K-6 program (which utilizes the Renzulli Enrichment Triad Model). The Odyssey of the Mind Program stresses creative thinking. Two special art classes are part of the G/T program. Mentorships have been arranged for some Native American students as has attendance at a special camp for gifted Native American students.

Contact and Address
Karen Davidson, G/T Coordinator
Hardin Public Schools
Elementary District No. 17H and High School
District No. 1
P. O. Box 310
Hardin, MT 59034
406/665-1408

Program Title
FOCUS/Challenge Gifted

Purpose/Goals
Identification of culturally diverse gifted students. Goals include helping students to:
1. Develop academic strengths;
2. Increase self-motivation;
3. Enhance student self-concept;
4. Encourage formal educational participation; and
5. Encourage setting of realistic and attainable career goals.

Population
Culturally diverse students: free or reduced lunch status, minority race, frequent school moves, or bilingualism.

Description
Assessment: Classroom teachers initially identify students from low economic or culturally diverse backgrounds not identified by standard district criteria. Assessment measures, including the Learning Style Identification Scale and the Atypical Gifted Form of the SOI Diagnostic Battery, are employed and an individual student profile is developed.

Service Delivery: Identified students participate in pull-out Challenge, Omnibus, or Junior Great Books, and summer Challenge classes.

Student Outcomes: In 1990-1991, 1,035 gifted students were included in the Challenge Talented Pool through FOCUS identification.

Contact and Address
Judy Hennig, Supervisor of Gifted/Talented Education
Gifted/Talented Education
Omaha Public Schools
3215 Cuming Street
Omaha, NE 68131
402/554-6265

Program Title
Gifted and Talented Education

Purpose/Goals
1. Use of multiple identification criteria;
2. Incorporation of divergent thinking into the instructional program;
3. Use of parent, teacher, and administrator nomination;
4. Utilization of continuous measures;
5. Inclusive rather than exclusive approach to identification;
6. Use of local norms for measuring giftedness;
7. Cost-effective process.

Population
Grades K-8

Description
Assessment: nomination, screening, and selection process.

Service Delivery: Services are based on the J. Renzulli Enrichment Triad model.

Contact and Address
Dr. Vilma Helms
Gifted/Talented Education
Dayton Public Schools
2013 West Third Street
Dayton, OH 45417
513/262-2770

State Questionnaire

A questionnaire was sent to all 50 states and U. S. territories seeking answers to the questions listed below. States were asked to circle the number that represented their response to each item. (Range: 5 = to a great extent to 1 = not at all.)

1. To what extent do the programs for students who are gifted in your state reflect principles of equality and pluralism?

2. To what degree does your state include the variable of low socioeconomic status in the process of identifying students for gifted programs?

3. To what extent does your state include the variable of race or ethnicity in the process of identifying students for gifted programs?

4. To what extent does your state use an *amalgam* of race and low socioeconomic status in the process of identifying students for gifted programs?

5. Which of the below most closely approximates the factors of "disadvantagement" utilized in your state definition for students who are gifted? (Check all that apply. If *b* is checked, go to question six; otherwise go to question seven.)

    a. Environmental factors
    b. Socioeconomic factors
    c. Linguistic factors
    d. Cultural differences
    e. Ethnicity status
    f. No inclusion of disadvantaged gifted considerations in state definition.

6. If your state includes low socioeconomic status (SES) in the process for selecting students for gifted programs, which of the following is used to define low SES?

    a. Bureau of Labor Statistics table of income based on household size
    b. Qualification for free or reduced lunch
    c. Qualification for Aid to Families with Dependent Children
    d. Other (please specify)

7. To what extent do the programs for students who are gifted in your state reflect expanded conceptions of giftedness beyond general intellectual ability, as discerned through IQ and achievement tests?

8. To what extent do programs for students who are gifted in your state use nonbiased assessment instruments in the identification process?

9. To what extent are the following techniques used in your state to identify students who are gifted?

   a. Nontraditional testing instruments (e.g., Ravens Progressive Matrices test, SOMPA)
   b. Observation techniques
   c. Teacher nominations
   d. Community nominations
   e. Parent nominations/interviews
   f. Peer nominations
   g. Self-nomination
   h. Creativity indices (e.g., Torrance Test, Structure of Intellect Learning Abilities Test, etc.)
   i. Leadership Skills Inventories
   j. Psychomotor Skills Inventories
   k. Student products (e.g., student essays, projects, etc.)
   l. Evaluation of pupil products by experts
   m. Case studies
   n. Learning style inventory
   o. Behavioral identification or adaptive behavior
   p. Norm-referenced tests
   q. Other (please list any additional procedures)

10. Check all of the approaches below that characterize programs in your state for students who are disadvantaged/gifted.

    a. Early intervention
    b. Academic programs (e.g., core content areas of language arts, mathematics, science, and social studies)
    c. Counseling programs
    d. Individual tutorials
    e. Mentorships
    f. Internships
    g. Arts program (e.g., visual arts, theater, music, dance)
    h. Creative programs (e.g., creative thinking and problem solving in various domains)
    i. Academic skill development (e.g., bridging)
    j. Process skill development (e.g., critical thinking, research, and problem solving)
    k. Test taking skills
    l. Acceleration (be content area or grade)
    m. Nontraditional placements (e.g., dual enrollment in high school/college, museology programs, work study)
    n. High school students in college courses
    o. Independent study
    p. Other

11. To what extent do you differentiate programs and services for your disadvantaged/gifted population from other gifted programs and services offered to advantaged gifted populations?

12. Check any of the following approaches used by your state to encourage funding for students who are disadvantaged/gifted.

    a. Set-asides
    b. Goals for disadvantaged participation
    c. Required documentation in state plan for a focus on students who are disadvantaged/gifted
    d. Identification standards that require that a portion of students who are gifted come from disadvantaged backgrounds
    e. Other (please specify).

13. Does your budget for gifted programs require a certain percentage of funds for students who are disadvantaged/gifted?

14. If your budget encourages a proportion of funding for students who are disadvantaged/gifted please indicate the percentage of this total funding.

15. If your funding model requires both state and local contributions, please indicate the percentage of funds required from each category on this issue.

16. Of other funding sources at the state level, what percentage of these funds are set aside for students who are disadvantaged/gifted? (Please indicate the funding source, amount of funds, and percentage.)

17. Have you developed program standards for students who are disadvantaged/gifted as a special category?

18. Are there initiatives in your state to monitor LEAs in their provision for specific services to learners who are disadvantaged/gifted? (If so, please cite relevant procedures or processes.)

19. Have you developed special materials, handbooks, and/or guidelines related to the learner who is disadvantaged/gifted ? (Please cite author, title, and attach copy.)

20. Can you provide data on the numbers of students who are disadvantaged/gifted being served in your state? (If yes, please specify total number served, total gifted population served in your state, number of districts serving learners who are disadvantaged/gifted, and total number of districts in your state.)

21. Additional comments.

Local School District Questionnaire

A questionnaire was sent to a selected group of local school districts (51) that were nominated by their state directors of gifted programs based on their program activity for at-risk gifted learners. Districts were asked to circle their response to each of the following items. On some items, districts were asked to complete an open-ended question.

1. Does your school district define learners who are disadvantaged/gifted? State the definition used.

2. Which of the factors listed below most closely approximates the factors of "disadvantagement" utilized by your district in finding and serving students in gifted programs who are disadvantaged? (Check all that apply.)

   a. Environmental factors
   b. Socioeconomic factors
   c. Linguistic factors
   d. Cultural differences
   e. Ethnicity status
   f. Other (please cite)

3. If your school district includes low socioeconomic status in the process for selecting students for gifted programs, which of the following is used to define low socioeconomic status?

   a. Bureau of Labor Statistics table of income based on household size
   b. Qualification for free or reduced lunch
   c. Qualification for Aid to Families with Dependent Children
   d. Other (please specify)

4. To what extent do the programs for gifted learners in your district reflect expanded conceptions of giftedness beyond general intellectual ability as discerned through IQ and achievement testing? (Range: 5 = to a great extent to 1 = not at all.)

5. To what extent do programs in your state for learners who are gifted use nonbiased assessment instruments in the identification process? (Range: 5 = to a great extent to 1 = not at all.)

6. Which of the following techniques are used in your district to identify students who are disadvantaged/gifted? (Check all that apply, and cite the form, instrument, inventory or process used.)

   a. Nontraditional testing instruments, (e.g., Ravens Progressive Matrices test, SOMPA). Cite names and attach copies of instruments used.
   b. Observation techniques

    c. Teacher nominations
    d. Community nominations
    e. Parent nominations/interview
    f.   Peer nominations
    g. Creativity Indices (e.g., Torrance Test, Structure of Intellect Learning Abilities Test, etc.)
    h. Leadership Skills Inventories
    i.   Psychomotor Skills Inventories
    j.   Student products (e.g., student essays, projects, etc.)
    k. Self-nominations
    l.   Case studies
    m. Behavioral identification or adaptive behavior
    n. Norm-referenced tests
    o. Other (please list any additional procedures).

7.   How many learners who are disadvantaged/gifted does your district serve? How many total gifted learners does your district serve?

8.   Check all of the approaches below that characterize your programs for learners who are disadvantaged/gifted.

    a. Early intervention programs
    b. Academic skill development
    c. Academic programs (e.g., in core content areas of language, mathematics, science, social studies)
    d. Process skill development (e.g., critical thinking, research, problem solving
    e. Counseling programs
    f.   Test-taking skills
    g. Individual tutorials
    h. Acceleration (by content area *or* grade)
    i.   Mentorships
    j.   Nontraditional placements (e.g., dual enrollment in high school/college, museology program, and work-study)
    k. Creative programs (e.g., creative thinking and problem-solving in various domains)
    l.   Independent study
    m. Other (please cite)

9.   Identify the grade levels at which you serve learners who are disadvantaged/gifted. (Check all that apply.)

10. To what extent do you differentiate programs and services for your disadvantaged/gifted population from programs and services offered to advantaged gifted populations? (Range: 5 = to a great extent to 1 = not at all.)

11. Do you perceive your students who are disadvantaged/gifted to exhibit the following characteristics *more* than your other gifted learners: (Check all that apply.)

a. Flexibility in thinking patterns
b. Erratic academic performance
c. Preference for oral over written tasks
d. Difficulty with homework completion
e. Procrastination over tasks
f. Preference for expressive activities
g. Quickness of warm-up
h. Exhibit risk-taking behavior in the classroom
i. Exhibit maturity
j. Need for confirmation of their abilities
k. Need for recognition for their accomplishments
l. Daily reinforcement for their work
m. Need for frequent feedback on progress

12. To what extent do your students who are disadvantaged/gifted display the following behaviors? (Range: 5 = to a great extent to 1 = not at all.) For how many disadvantaged gifted students is the stated behavior displayed? (Range: 5 = most to 1 = none.)

Elementary and Secondary
a. Making ideas concrete
b. Understanding consequences for present behavior
c. Generalizing
d. Developing social interaction behavior with diverse groups
e. Valuing their own ideas
f. Working toward a goal
g. Organizing time

Secondary
h. Seeing themselves in adult roles
i. Thinking about life in college
j. Planning for the future beyond one year

13. To what extent does your gifted program respond to key aspects in the background experiences of learners who are disadvantaged/gifted by providing the following: (Range: 5 = to a great extent to 1 = not at all.)

a. Learning experiences representing a multicultural perspective
b. Use of nontraditional family models as positive examples
c. Specific study of cultures of which disadvantaged students are representative
d. Monetary support for enrichment activities beyond the school
e. Parent awareness programs that focus on strategies for assisting bright students in the home
f. Use of biography to instill pride and identification with sex, race, and background of learners

14. Research has suggested that the following kinds of interventions are successful for learners who are disadvantaged. Do you feel you

employ these strategies in your gifted program and do you apply them differentially to students who are disadvantaged?

a. Provisions for preschool experiences
b. Parent participation
c. Direct service to families
d. Small adult-child ratio
e. Structured learning environments
f. Emphasis on reading instruction
g. Motivated principal and teacher shared leadership
h. Use of diagnostic-prescriptive teaching
i. Concern for student learning style
j. Strong use of praise and encouragement
k. Verbal recognition of student ideas and feelings
l. Use of creative writing, role playing and choral reading
m. Use of ethnic literature

15. In your opinion, what important successes and problems of students who are disadvantaged/gifted are being overlooked by educators? (List the top three successes and top three problems.)

16. Have you developed evaluation standards for programs for learners who are disadvantaged/gifted? If so, are they the same as for all gifted programs?

17. What special approaches do you use in evaluating programs and services for students who are disadvantaged/gifted? (Check all that apply.)

a. Interviews
b. Case studies
c. Longitudinal follow-up (2 years or more)
d. Questionnaires to students
e. Questionnaires to parents
f. Questionnaires to teachers
g. Process observation (i.e., check list completed by teacher or outside evaluator)
h. Pre-post assessments
i. Other (specify)

18. Based on the evaluation approach(es) you use, how effective do you perceive your current programs and services to be for this population? (Range: 5 = very effective to 1 = not at all effective.)

19. Have you developed special materials, handbooks, or guidelines related to students who are disadvantaged/gifted? (If yes, please cite author, title, and attach copy.)

20. Have any longitudinal follow-up studies been conducted of graduates from your gifted program who are disadvantaged?

21. If yes, what types of findings have been recorded?

22. Please indicate the appropriate percentage (%) or indicate "don't know" for each category of information on learners who are disadvantaged/gifted who graduated from your school district over the past one to five years,

    a. Took Advanced Placement classes
    b. Took AP exams
    c. Received college credits for AP coursework
    d. Attended a two-year college
    e. Attended a four-year college
    f. Attended post-high school performing arts academy (e.g., Julliard, Cranbrook, etc.)
    g. Attended a selective four-year college
    h. Attended college out-of-state
    i. Graduated from a four-year institution
    j. Entered a professional school (e.g., law, medicine)
    k. Entered the business world (e.g., accounting, management)
    l. Attended graduate school or advanced degree programs.

23. Other comments

CEC Products Related to the Education of Gifted and Talented Students

Call for the most current price information
703/620-3660
Send orders to
The Council for Exceptional Children, Dept. 10950
1920 Association Drive, Reston, VA 22091